Praise for *In Spite of Everything*

"Raw, funny, searingly honest and electrifyingly intelligent. As a field guide to the beat-up, busted heart of Generation X, it's damn near definitive. Thomas solves the mystery of her devastating divorce—and the emotional catastrophe that defines a generation."

—LEV GROSSMAN, author of *The Magicians*

"This smart and emotionally mighty memoir will show you how every family of divorce is unhappy in ways we can all relate to, learn from, cry about, and (after reading such a great book) transcend. Sad and funny, *In Spite of Everything* is the first book to dissect, with scientific definitiveness, the Busted-Marriage Generation. It also tells a very moving personal story with real beauty."

—DARIN STRAUSS, author of *Half a Life*

"At once a literate and poignant memoir and incisive journalistic illumination of the cult of domestic consumption, *In Spite of Everything* is a remarkable and moving study of an American generation's uneasy search for home."

—WELLS TOWER, author of *Everything Ravaged, Everything Burned*

"This book is brave, startling, and profoundly moving, and I could not put it down."

—JOANNA HERSHON, author of *The German Bride* and *Swimming*

"Harrowing, hilarious, and profoundly wise, *In Spite of Everything* is the work of a supreme talent and an emotional daredevil, a woman courageous enough to reveal every scar that lines her heart."

—BRENDAN I. KOERNER, author of *Now the Hell Will Start*

"Honest, riveting and illuminating. . . . An indelible portrait not only of a family, but of an entire generation shaped by loneliness. Breathtakingly beautiful from start to finish."
— LISA DIERBECK, author of *One Pill Makes You Smaller*

"In *In Spite of Everything*, Susan Gregory Thomas goes way beyond American pop culture's cute, run-of-the-mill bromides about marriage and parenting and gives us a work that's shot through with a stark and clarifying light of honesty. It is an inspiring book—and often an uproariously funny one, too. *In Spite of Everything* establishes Thomas as one of the most important new voices in American writing."
— JEFF GORDINIER, author of *X Saves the World*

"As a memoir, *In Spite of Everything* is both raw and smart; as a generational analysis, it is spot on—culturally, economically, and psychologically. This is an engaging and fast-paced memoir, and a generational portrait for those who refuse to be categorized."
— LISA CHAMBERLAIN, author of *Slackonomics: Generation X in the Age of Creative Destruction*

"*In Spite of Everything* is a profound emotional history of the last forty years. Susan Gregory Thomas is the expert on Generation X's emotional fallout. All recovering latchkey kids should read this book."
— ADA CALHOUN, author of *Instinctive Parenting: Trusting Ourselves to Raise Good Kids*

"An engrossing memoir, and a deeply moving and personal tale of divorce, love, motherhood, and what makes us who we are."
— MARIAN FONTANA, author of *A Widow's Walk*

ALSO BY SUSAN GREGORY THOMAS

Buy, Buy Baby: How Consumer Culture Manipulates
Parents and Harms Young Minds

IN SPITE OF EVERYTHING

RANDOM HOUSE
NEW YORK

IN SPITE OF EVERYTHING

A MEMOIR

Susan Gregory Thomas

In Spite of Everything is a work of nonfiction. Certain names have been changed in order to disguise the identities of the persons discussed. Any resulting resemblance to persons living or dead is entirely coincidental and unintentional.

Published in the United States by Random House,
an imprint of The Random House Publishing Group,
a division of Random House, Inc., New York.

RANDOM HOUSE and colophon are
registered trademarks of Random House, Inc.

Portions of this book were originally published as articles by
Babble.com and MSNBC.com.

Library of Congress Cataloging-in-Publication Data
Thomas, Susan Gregory.
In spite of everything : a memoir / by Susan Gregory Thomas.
p. cm.
Includes bibliographical references.
ISBN 978-1-4000-6882-1
eBook ISBN 978-1-58836-946-8
1. Thomas, Susan Gregory.   2. Thomas, Susan Gregory—Marriage.
3. Thomas, Susan Gregory—Divorce.   4. Divorced women—United States—
Biography.   I. Title.
CT275.T5566A3 2011
306.89'3092—dc22
[B]   2010043104

Printed in the United States of America on acid-free paper

www.atrandom.com

246897531

First Edition

Book design by Karin Batten

For my family
(and a little bit for Eminem)

CONTENTS

PROLOGUE:
MORE THAN THIS

Every generation has its life-defining moment. If you want to find out what it was for a member of the Greatest Generation, you ask: "Where were you when Hitler invaded France?" or "Where were you on D-Day?" If you want to find out what it was for a Baby Boomer, there are three possible questions: "Where were you when Kennedy was shot?" or "Where were you when you heard about Kent State?" or "Where were you when the Watergate story broke?"

For most of my generation—Generation X—there is only one question: "When did your parents get divorced?"

Our lives have been framed by the answer. Ask us. We remember everything.

My dad left in the early spring of 1981, while my mother was leading a school trip to England. While she was away that week, Dad was in charge. I was twelve; my brother, Ian, was nine.

On the first night, Dad called to say he was running late, that he might not be there by dinnertime. We'd never had to make dinner for ourselves before, but I knew that Mom had a stash of Stouffer's French bread pizzas in the freezer. Unsettled, Ian and I were nonetheless united in one thought: unmediated access to TV. We sat on the floor of our parents' room, watched *Magnum, P.I.,* and ate the pizzas. We ended up falling asleep on the rug.

When we woke up the next morning, our father was lying on top of the bed in his dark gray pinstripe Brooks Brothers suit, his standard investment management uniform. The whole room smelled of Dad: scotch, sweat, and shaving cream. His white dress shirt was pressed to his chest like wet tissue paper; his face was dusted with unfamiliar salt-white whiskers. Ian and I looked at each other, scared. Dad was a perennial early riser: up hours before anyone else, impeccably shaved and dressed—reading the paper and drinking coffee by 5:30 A.M. It was now after eight; we had to be at school, sitting at our desks, by 8:25. Ian and I swapped staccato whispers over our father's body, when suddenly he opened his eyes, webbed with raw capillaries. "Let's go," Dad growled, and got up immediately. We followed, mute. He drove us to our respective schools without a word.

The second night, no phone call. It was cold in the house; usually, it took two furnaces to heat it, and I didn't know how to turn them on. I called our current babysitter, a college student at Villanova University named Carol. I told her that my dad wasn't home and asked if she could call him. There was a pause on the line. Then she said she'd be right over. She was there in fifteen minutes.

The next afternoon, I came home from school and no one was there. My brother had been taken to Cub Scouts by someone's mother, I think, and Carol was still in classes. I was in the kitchen prying frozen orange juice concentrate out of its canister when my dad pulled up. I looked out the kitchen window, waiting for him to get out of the car. A few minutes went by. I went outside.

He was sitting in the driver's seat of his sports car, a plastic tumbler of scotch in his hand. He was wearing the same clothes. He didn't look at me. I ripped a hangnail off my thumb and chewed it. Finally, I opened the door and got in. "Hi, Dad," I said.

He didn't say anything. The ashtray was open; there were three cigarette butts inside, each O'ed with pink lipstick. He tilted the tumbler back, slipped the scotch into his mouth, opened the car door, got out, and popped the trunk. My thumb had bled onto the sleeve of my white school shirt.

When I came around to the back of the car, I saw that there was a case of scotch in the trunk. Dad was pouring from a newly opened bottle into his tumbler. He silently screwed the cap back on and clinked the bottle into the box. He chugged it back, eyes closed. He set the glass on the hood.

"Everything okay here?" he asked.

"Carol came," I said, sucking at my thumb.

"Can she stay?"

"I don't know."

"I have to go on a business trip," he said. "As it turns out." He slammed the trunk shut and finally looked at me.

"I have to go now," he said. "Call if you need me." He squeezed my shoulder, got in the car, and drove out of the driveway.

After a few moments, I sat down. I was wearing the navy blue tunic uniform of my all-girls' school, and loose driveway pebbles stuck to my bloomer-covered bottom and the backs of my thighs. I wrapped the belt of my tunic around my wound. It was cold and wet still, early spring. The edges of the front yard were flanked by forsythia, which were just budding Crayola yellow. I'd never had his number to begin with.

"Whatever happens, we're never going to get divorced."

Over the course of sixteen years, I said that often to my husband, Cal, especially after our two daughters were born. No marital scenario would ever become so bleak or hopeless as to compel me, even for a moment, to embed my children in the torture of my own split family. After my dad left (with his secretary, who would become his second of three wives), the world as my brother and I had known it ended. Just like that. My mother, formerly a regal, erudite figure, shape-shifted into a phantom in a sweaty nightgown and matted hair, howling on the floor of our gray-carpeted playroom. Ian, a sweet, doofusy boy, grew into a sad, glowering giant, barricaded in his room with dark comic books, graphic novels, and computer games. I would spend the rest of middle and high school getting into a lot of surprisingly bad trouble in suburban Philadelphia: chain-smoking, doing drugs, getting kicked out of schools, ending my senior year in a psychiatric ward. Our dad was gone. He immediately moved five states away, with his new wife and her four kids. Whenever Ian and I saw him, which was, per his preference, rarely, he grew more and more to embody Darth Vader: a brutal machine encasing raw human guts. Growing up, Ian and I were often left to our own devices, circumstances that did not so much teach us how to take care of ourselves as simply how to survive. We dealt. We developed detached, sarcastic riffs on "our messed-up childhood."

We weren't the only ones. The particular memorabilia that comprise each family's unhappiness are always different, but a lot of our friends were going through the same basic stuff at the time—and a lot of people our age we *didn't* know were, too. The divorce epidemic of the 1970s and '80s wiped out nearly half our generation.

According to a recent study of generational differences, Generation X—those of us born between 1965 and 1980—"went through its all-important, formative years as one of the least parented, least nurtured generations in U.S. history." U.S. census and other data report that almost half of all Generation X children's families split; 40 percent were latchkey kids. People my parents' age all say things like "Of *course* you'd feel devastated by divorce, honey—it was a horrible, disorienting time for you as a child! Of *course* you wouldn't want it for yourself and your family, but sometimes it's better for everyone that parents part ways; everyone is happier." Such sentiments bring to mind a set of statistics that has stuck with me: In 1962, half of all adult women believed that parents in bad marriages should stay together for the children's sake; by 1980, only one in five felt that way. A child in the 1980s faced twice the risk of parental divorce as a Boomer child in the mid-1960s. "Four-fifths of [those] divorced adults profess to being happier afterward," the authors write, "but a majority of their children feel otherwise." *

But a majority of their children feel otherwise. There is something intolerable about that clause. Because, although I realize this view is lunatic and hyperbolic, there is still something in me that feels that to get divorced is to enact *Medea:* the wailing, murderously bereft mother; the cold father protecting his pristine new family; the children: dead.

Not me. I married my husband because he was the most wonderful, reliable, stable person I had ever met. When my children were born a few years later, I stopped being cool, or what I thought was cool, because I fell in love with them so completely that my cool circuit blew out on the spot. As a mother, this became my foxhole prayer: Please, please, Whatever Karmic Force There Is, do not let divorce happen to *my* children. Divorce didn't just evoke a sense of a sad, disruptive period, a portrait of parents yelling, children numbly munching frozen pizzas in front of TV cartoons. It had been scorched earth. The Bomb.

How can a person find herself doing precisely what she has built

---

* William Strauss and Neil Howe, *Generations: The History of America's Future, 1584 to 2069* (New York: Morrow, 1991), p. 324.

her life's framework to *avoid*? As the daughter of a onetime classicist, and a former English major and theater geek myself, I knew the answer as well as anyone: Look no farther than Oedipus. But my feeling—really, my absolute certainty—was, again: *not me*. And yet, there I was. After sixteen years of life with Cal, I found myself without warning in the one place I had vowed never to be. Here I was sitting at a cozy-chic restaurant in Park Slope, Brooklyn, crying that I was miserable in our relationship, had been for years, and hearing Cal respond that he, too, was miserable and regretted that we hadn't split up a decade earlier.

It seemed that the light blew out. My field of vision narrowed to his dinner plate, blown with bits of rice and desiccated meat. There was one thought: *I am here. In spite of everything.*

It is a hard truism that each generation is shaped by its war. The Greatest Generation (1929–43) was forged by World War II; Baby Boomers (1944–64) were defined by Vietnam and the civil rights and antiwar movements. Generation X's war, I would argue, was the ultimate war at home: divorce. We didn't get Purple Hearts or red badges of courage, nothing that could be culturally shared or healed. Our injuries were private, secret, solitary. Our generation's drug use—unlike that of Baby Boomers, who favored the grandiose highs of psychedelics and, later, cocaine—revolved around heroin, Percocet, Oxycontin: painkillers. Outdoors, there was crack, AIDS, homelessness, racial conflict, Reaganomics. Indoors was the mall, in roving packs. Home? Alone, watching program-length commercials. "More than this," crooned Bryan Ferry in Roxy Music's eponymous eighties lullaby, "there is nothing." The novel of our decade: *Less Than Zero*. The protagonist's central crisis strikes when he encounters a billboard for a resort that reads DISAPPEAR HERE.

We did not disappear; we just stuffed the void with whatever we could grab. Many of us, including me, thrashed our way out of adolescence and worked our asses off to get as far away as possible from that *terroir* of existential fear. We developed crusts to cover our raw centers. Sociologists have shown how the effects of the mass divorces of the 1980s linger subtly but powerfully in our behavior as adults now, in our struggle to do everything differently.

Without a safe home to belong to, we still see ourselves as the misfits, the outsiders, the snickering critics who see through everyone else's pretenses. Terminal uniqueness, it turns out, is a hallmark of Generation X. The insistence that you are different, cannot be stuck with any label, are impossible to categorize, is a phenomenon that marketers, somewhat hilariously, call "focus group of one." Try your own. Start a conversation with people our age about Generation X, and see if they don't respond with something like "Exactly *who* decided that I was in 'Generation X' *anyway*?" or "I've never paid attention to those kinds of sociological generalizations." But according to studies, we *do* conform to sociological generalizations in that we refuse to acknowledge them, even as we conform to them.

First, market research shows that we all bristle at being called "Gen X" (funny: "I Am Not a Target Market" was a chapter in Douglas Coupland's *Generation X: Tales for an Accelerated Culture*, published in 1991). Indeed, we still have a jaundiced view of authority, just as we did as adolescents. We're still self-reliant; after all, we've been making our own dinner since we were six years old. We never counted on gold watches or pensions; we recalibrated ourselves and our careers as often as the economy morphed. We came to the whole idea of love after we'd been battered around like middle-aged divorcées—and when we actually found it, we cleaved to it. Love meant everything. It certainly did to me. It was my vulnerable little secret. I may have seemed jaded, but I was, after all, a kid needing love, security, and attention—the very things my parents had been too distracted and overwhelmed to offer.

So I, like many of us, made it. But I, like, I'd bet, many of us, unconsciously banked on the fuzzy logic that arrival in adulthood would somehow summon a mystical force that would seal up that gaping hole forever, like the giant boulder rolling over the cave entrance in *Aladdin*. It worked, for a while. Until we became parents.

It is a well-worn axiom that if you want to learn what is unhealed from your own childhood, have children. In psychological terms, this is known as a "narcissistic injury" or "narcissistic wound." Parents have always had specific nightmares that plague them in peculiar ways. For some, it is the unquenchable fear that their child may be picked on by stronger or meaner kids; others are terrorized by drowning scenarios; still others imagine the horrors of sexual exploitation. All such nightmares, many psychologists would argue, are rooted in the parents' own childhood fears. For Generation X, I think, it is the dread of abandonment that keeps us up at night—dread stemming from having been utterly alone ourselves as kids. It makes sense, then, that to allow our own marriages to end in divorce is to live out our worst possible childhood fear, but, more horrifying, it is to inflict the unthinkable on those we love and want to protect most: our children. We would be slashing open our own wounds and then turning the knife on our babies. To think of it is impossible.

Nobody puts it quite like Alice Miller, the renowned psychologist who—in her seminal text on the subject, *The Drama of the Gifted Child*—describes those of us who sustained such childhood wounds: "They are driven by unconscious memories and by repressed feelings and needs that determine nearly everything they do or fail to do."* When we become adults, marriage, with children, becomes the center of our universe. It *is* the world. Market research has shown that

---

* *The Drama of the Gifted Child: The Search for the True Self* (New York: Basic Books, 1997), p. 2.

we won't ask our own mothers for child-rearing advice because we feel they failed as mothers, and we've decided we're going to walk the polar opposite line. Having grown up without a stable home, we pour everything we have into giving our children the homiest possible home, no matter how many sacrifices that means along the way. Our lives center around our own kids' childhoods, around saving them from the smallest pain. Survey says: Despite our hardened exteriors, our crunchy crust, Gen-X moms are all completely, utterly attached to our children. We would rather err on the side of being too close, too involved, too loving than repeat our own parents' sin of neglect. Scan any Gen-X mommy blog, and you'll find them all variations on a theme: the cool, maverick mama with the giant, attachment-parenting heart. A photo of Mom's arm tattooed graffiti-style with her kids' names. The combat boots and the nursing bra. The adorable baby girl in her Clash onesie. You get the idea.

A lot of this is a result of the parenting style with which so many of us were raised: "benign neglect." It is a recognizable outcropping of the "good-enough mother" ideal proposed by the great child psychologist D. W. Winnicott, in which the imperfectly conscientious mother does a better job than the "perfect" one by allowing her child to develop as an independent being rather than smothering him with attention. If you are an X parent, you have likely heard your Boomer parents' thoughts on the subject. The salient points are "When we were kids, our mothers just told us to be home by dinnertime" and "We would just hop on our bikes and roam the neighborhood" or "play stickball in the street"—and how sad it is that "kids today just don't get that kind of freedom" because it is "*so* important to their development."*

But what Boomers often omit from these object lessons is that in

---

* In my experience, such reminiscences always seem tacked with punctuation marks subtly denoting superiority, allowing plenty of white space for the implied conclusion: "And maybe *that's* why we've occupied the lead roles on the national stage since we hit puberty."

the 1950s and '60s, their mothers were at home to tell them to get on their bikes, and the reason they had to be at home by dinnertime is that their fathers would be expecting the whole family to sit down together. As Dr. Spock had advised that generation of parents, there were clear house rules, no spanking, attentiveness to the children. By contrast, for most of us who grew up in the 1970s and '80s, life at home revolved around a pattern of benign neglect that looked something like this: We watched Saturday morning cartoons and *Brady Bunch* reruns while playing with *Star Wars* and *Transformers* action figures or Strawberry Shortcake and My Pretty Pony dolls. Our parents got divorced, and when our moms went to work, they gave us the house keys so that we could let ourselves in after school. We helped ourselves to something in the orange category of snack, like Cheetos and Doritos, or in the white—Top Ramen noodles, Pringles, Fluffernutter sandwiches—while we watched ABC After-School Specials like *My Dad Lives in a Downtown Hotel* and *The Boy Who Drank Too Much.* When Mom came home, she was too tired to cook, so it was either TV dinners at home or stuffed potato skins at Houlihan's. We saw our dads every other weekend, and after they bought us more *Star Wars* stuff, sometimes they'd take us to their single-guy apartments, which looked like the last day of a Macy's clearance sale. Lunch? Bennigan's.

Where was the "benign" part in this "benign neglect"? Friends and I often joke that whereas Baby Boomers' mothers actually did practice Winnicott's counsel, our own mothers just went for "neglect neglect." To this, our mothers often bring up feminism and all the important ways in which the women's movement made it possible for their daughters to go to college and launch real careers. No one would wish to minimize this effort. After all, most of us who have had a higher education and a career to go with it—whether Boomer or Xer—can affirm that we would not wish the repressive delirium of the Feminine Mystique or Yellow Wallpaper on any woman. Neither would we want to yoke men with the albatross of disaffected breadwinner. Yet what the X mother cannot shake is this: In the realm of the child, whose worst fear is to be alone and unprotected, such feminist affirmations mean nothing. If children are alone and unprotected, they are damaged—period.

In other words, for "benign neglect" to function as a parenting style, there must be the presumption of "benign" for children to reap the developmental benefits of "neglect"—and "benign" amounts to the security of knowing that they are *not* really on their own, having to fend for themselves. This is why, according to many child development experts, alone and unprotected is the chief condition of fairy-tale protagonists—and why they must find parental surrogates to prevail. Where, after all, would Cinderella be without her fairy god-mother? What would have become of Snow White without her gnomish octogenarians? X mothers know that Cinderella would likely have been recast as Courtney Love, whimpering to a succession of palace houseboys: *Go on, take everything, take everything, I want you to!* Snow White might have been recast in the sweet, pretty form of Kurt Cobain, lost in the forest: *All alone is all we are, all alone is all we are.*

Call us helicopter parents, call us neurotically attached, but we are *not* going to inflict such wounds on *our* children. And for me, the fundamental premise of wound avoidance was simple: No divorce.

Yet, as Sophocles has reminded us for more than two thousand years, one can design one's life around preventing the very scenario that eventually unfolds via one's own hand in spite of everything. Looking back on it, it seems obvious now that just about everything I ever did in my life was either a response to my own parents' divorce or a preemptive move geared to stave off my own. I became involved in "relationships" at a preternaturally early age in an effort to supply fatherly attention and protection with boyfriends; I drank and drugged to fend off the nagging, existential terror of solipsism; I worked like an animal to attract surrogate parental attention, as well as to try to caulk up the hole in my gut; I married the kindest, most stable person I'd ever known to secure kindness and stability in my own empty but turbulent universe—and to ensure that our children would never know anything of that void; I nursed, loved, read to, and lolled about with my babies—completely restructured and reimagined my career—so that they would be secure, happy, attended to; my husband and I made the happiest, comfiest nest possible; we worked as a team; we loved our kids; we did everything right, better than right. And yet divorce came. In spite of everything. In spite of my not having seen it bearing down on me, us, from light-years away. Oedipus didn't know that the stranger he had killed in the road years before was his father until he had already been long and happily married to the woman who turned out to be his mother. In spite of everything.

This is an account of a sharp turn in life I never expected to take. I found myself wrestling with the very decisions that I never thought I would think of making but that I found myself having to make, with the nearly superhuman attempt to keep life as gentle and undisrupted as possible for our children—essentially, the effort to reverse-engineer childhood karma. My story is a meditation on our generation and the fallout from our parents' divorces, looking at what those divorces did to us, why it now feels to us that shielding our kids from any kind of pain is a life-or-death proposition, what happens when real pain happens anyway—and what it is like to inhabit an entirely new world.

Before the events of the past five years, I could never even have contemplated some of the questions I've been forced to confront. Namely, is it possible to survive the explosive upending of divorce without inflicting permanent wounds on our own children? Is it possible, by surviving it as adults, that our own injuries might actually begin to heal? *All alone is all we are,* whimpered our sweet, lost, sad, fallen hero. Our fear is that "alone" *is* the central truth that lies at the heart of the universe, and that if we cannot provide them with an unimpeachably happy childhood, our children will be forced to stare into that void by themselves, too.

But what if that isn't true? What if there *is* more than this? What if the only truly perfect gem that we can really keep and share with our children is that none of us is alone—that they can remain loved and secure, in spite of everything?

IN SPITE OF EVERYTHING

———•◆◆•———

ONE

LOUDER THAN BOMBS:
CHILDHOOD

When I was about four, my parents decided to make several home improvements. Back then, it seemed that every Berkeley family we knew had a deck on which the grown-ups—the mothers in their seventies wrap dresses and the dads in their weekend jeans—would sit drinking sangria and discussing Nixon, Bob Dylan, and public education while the kids mucked around in the playroom or tiny backyard in their school-made tie-dyes and Sears Toughskins. My mother had particular ideas about adding our own deck and playroom, ideas that involved French doors, window seats with giant storage drawers, and textured linoleum flooring. Although she was an academic—at the time, in graduate school at U.C. Berkeley, furiously at work on her dissertation—my mother nonetheless loved to work with professionals to help her make the right decisions about interior design and clothes.

My dad, for his part, had definite ideas about the second-floor room that was to be added: my room. Or, rather, he had one definite idea. My room had to have a skylight, and my bed was to be positioned directly beneath it. "Suze, as the official Little Dipper and Pleiades finder, you need the right tools," said my dad, who had conferred on me a special status for my knack for spotting these constellations in the night sky. "Furthermore, you may find, as I do, old pal, that you do your best star contemplation alone."

I remember two things vividly from that time. The first is that on the opening day of the renovation job, the construction guys left the French doors open while they were digging up the backyard to build the deck. I forgot that the ground outside was gone and walked right out into the pit, gashing open the bottom of my jaw on rocky debris. I had to go to the emergency room for stitches, and the remaining nettlefish-like scars still undergird the dimple on my chin. My mother was distraught and flailing, cracking her knuckles antsily and spraying me with Bactine. My dad, an ice climber by avocation, was a little more laid-back. He crouched down and took a look at the jagged green threads knitting my skin together. "You're tough as nails, Suze-o," he grinned.

The second thing I remember is lying in bed beneath the skylight. It was long and rectangular, and I would align my body with it at bedtime. My mother usually came in first, to read me poetry, often "The Highwayman" by Alfred Noyes. She would lean over my bed, throatily whispering, eyes wide with menace. After my mother had read this or another poem selected for stimulating a sense of cadence, Dad would come in. We would look up at the night sky and think. It occurs to me now that I never thought about what he was thinking; I guess I was too little to think that we were separate. What I thought was: Here are the stars; they are beautiful and strange; Dad is with me.

There is also something that I do not remember, but that I remember my parents worrying about at the time: As a young child, I was a chronic sleepwalker. I would not just roam into my parents' room or into the kitchen but actually walk *out* of the house and down the street to our family friends' house, ring the doorbell until one of the groggy adults answered, toddle into their living room, curl up on a sofa, and go back to sleep. The bewildered parent would call our house, and Dad would come scoop me up and take me back home.

The conflation of these events has always struck a primal chord in my sense of my own beginnings. Everyone has his own Genesis, the creation myth that allegorizes the idiom of his early childhood. But children, like all orthodox adherents, are literal thinkers, and, like native peoples, provincial ones. The universe originated in their homes and neighborhoods, and all the figures and fixtures therein are singular, monolithic, and mystical. Proust and Piaget said as much. A magnolia tree growing in the front yard, for example, is The Magnolia Tree; its gray polished bark is crinkled in a distinctive elderly-elephant-knee pattern where the first branch forks off from the trunk. A big slide at the playground is The Big Slide, a high diving board at the local pool is The High Dive. Such structures, which seem generic to parents, are the Everests, Denalis, Ulurus, Shiprocks of their children's aboriginal dreamtime. The children know every crack and contour of them all, have practiced strategies for mastering them, each child emerging as the mythical hero of her own folktale once that mission has been accomplished.

As a person gets older, however, these things present as personal archetypes, themes. One's life, it seems, plays out as variations on them.

Room. Poems. Gash. Sleepwalking. Stars. Ice.
Dad.

There is a giant so-called reference book called *The Secret Language of Birthdays,* which catalogs every day of the year and offers an astrological analysis of people born on that day. Whenever I see it at Barnes & Noble or on someone's coffee table, I sheepishly crack it open and look up everyone I've met since the last time I scoured it to see how it pigeonholes them. One of the neatest, and also one of the most idiotic, things about it is that each day gets its own headline, which is supposed to capture that person's astrological essence. Of course, they're often wrong. Mine, for example, is "The Day of the Boss," which is, as I am sure my younger brother would confirm, not correct. My dad's, however, is "The Day of Laughter and Tears." When I read that for the first time, I closed the book.

I am not someone who invests the portfolio in horoscopes, but I relish the feeling of cosmic symmetry when they seem to be on point, and if there ever was such a thing as a Gemini, that archetype could not have found a more impeccably corporeal landing than in the dual nature of Dugal Thomas. All Gemini's twin aspects were writ large in my dad: good/evil; contemplative/foolhardy; kinetic/paralyzed; expansive/hermetic; funny/brooding. You never knew which you were going to get. This is, as adult children later learn, one of the textbook characteristics of alcoholics. Knowing this explains a good deal, but in my experience, it doesn't do much to help significantly on the ground. As a child, even as a comprehending adult, all you are ever certain of is that any encounter will imprint you with either fear or delight. I was one of the lucky ones—at least until I was ten, it was unequivocally of delight.

Partly, this had to do with my mom. Although she very much wanted a baby, Mom was not, I think, prepared for the reality of having one. She was extremely anxious when I was born. She is this way constitutionally (as am I), but she also had a number of other very real weights pressing down on her at that time. For one thing, my parents—both New Yorkers—had just moved to California so that my mother could attend Cal's Ph.D. program in English Renaissance literature. For another, she had married my father only a year and a half before, after dating him for a handful of months—this directly on the heels of a disastrous nine-year marriage to her college boyfriend (note that my mom went to college—Wellesley—at sixteen), an intense and acerbic young man who had graduated at the top of his class from the Groton School, Harvard College, and Harvard Law School and who had competed with, shamed, and degraded her as much as he had idolized her. In my father she saw a charming, light-footed chap who had graduated with a straight-C average from Harvard; who was as much a painter, photographer, and naturalist as he was a patriot, a mountain climber, a guy's guy. Who also idolized her. He loved that she was tall and leggy, and for my mother—who, to this day, is self-conscious and klutzy and combats chronic back pain because of her height—his flattery was ambrosial. He loved how brilliant she was, and for my mother—who had spent a lifetime trying to impress her exacting parents, and then her ex-husband, with academic achievement—his praise was a lullaby. He loved that she was so lost and needy; she loved that he loved it. Of course he would support her going to graduate school—piece of cake! Of course they should have a baby right away—no time like the present! My dad made everything look so exciting, fun, easy. His trademark lines were: "So, I have an idea," and "Whatever you want—I'm easy!" Beware of peddlers with magic beans.

So there they were, three thousand miles from most of their friends and family, starting out on their exciting, fun, easy life. And you can tell from photos of that period that life was exactly like that for them then—certainly, I never witnessed them so goofy and huggy with each other. They looked relaxed and gorgeous, my mother's black hair, high cheekbones, and model stature glamorizing my dad's jocky, redheaded boyishness. But when I was born, in November 1968, fun and easy came to a grinding halt.

This is invariably true when a baby enters the household, even if you're over the moon about him. As every parent knows all too well, babies' needs are so constant and urgent that life is instantly more intense and demanding than you ever imagined it could be. It is fun for some, perhaps, but life with your first baby is not easy for anyone.

Especially for my mother. First of all, she was expecting someone else—a boy, for one thing. But, while embarrassed by her first fumble on maternal instincts, she was delighted with a girl. The first thing she said post-delivery was: "Her name is Susan Gregory, and we're going to read Milton together!" At least the first part was true. My mother's mother is from the South, where matrilineal naming traditions are common. On my nana's side of the family, the tradition was to name the eldest daughter of the eldest daughter "Susan Gregory" plus the last name of the infant's father. So I was the sixth in an unbroken line of eldest daughters having girls first. But I was different.

Nana was the first to see it. "This child is a redhead," she declared, on her first visit. "And she has blue eyes." My mother stiffened, irritated by her mother's hubristic prophecy. "Oh, Mother, don't be ridiculous," she sniffed. "She has black hair and brown eyes, like all the Susan Gregories. And look at her legs—she'll be tall, too." Nana shook her head. After a few weeks, when my true coloring began to emerge, it became obvious that Nana was right: I was a blue-eyed redhead. And, as it turned out, I was compact and athletic. Just like my dad.

Second, it wasn't just that I wasn't the baby my mother was expecting that compounded her anxiety. It's that I *was* a baby. People try to tell you what it's going to be like to have one, but there's no way you can understand it until you yourself have your own— whether you give birth or adopt. Some people are totally gaga over babies right away and squirm gleefully at their every belch and wiggle. Some people regard the newborn period as an endurance trial and are much more relaxed and happy once the baby can sit up, at around six months old. Some people are just not into babies, period. I'm not sure into which bunker my mother thought she would be slotted, but she found out right away that she was not only a member of that last troop, but also its leader. My mother was not, is not, a baby person.

For starters, there was the whole physicality of it. For a tall, physically unfit woman, pregnancy is extra hard on the back; she had to take pain medication for it. This may be why she didn't breast-feed, but she probably wouldn't have considered it at any rate. It would have felt unpalatable and unseemly to her. She may have been a grad student at Berkeley in the late sixties, but make no mistake: Pixie Thomas was, is, no earth mama. While she is no society matron either, my mother likes the fancy (as do I). She is a strictly Ferragamo flats, Yves Saint Laurent knit top, and Chanel lipstick woman. My mother was just plain different. Different from me, different from the other moms.

For one thing, she not only worked, she also did not really cook or bake unless there was a grown-up dinner party. For another thing, she didn't look anything like anyone else's mother. Where I grew up, near the Berkeley Hills, it was not the hippie but the cute tennis-skirt-wearing woman who was the reigning benevolent despot. My mother was the anti-Californian: intense, intimidating, anxious, bookish, hyperbolic, unathletic. She was not an officer of the PTA. She did not have a straight blond bob but obstreperously cork-screwed black hair. She was nine miles high of blindingly reflective white skin in a bathing suit, which was, like the hair, black. As a child, I sensed that the other California moms regarded her with an uneasy combination of inferiority, discomfort, and mockery. I figured that's how they must view me, too (minus the inferiority).

Although my parents did host festive dinner parties to which children came, we did not have many children over to our house outside of the close friends who lived down the street. But even so, ours was definitely not the "play" house. The walls were not decorated, like those of other Berkeley houses, with abstract artwork or Latin American wall hangings but were lined, floor to ceiling, with books—not ordinary paperbacks but, as my friend Ben said, "smart books." And it was messy. One of my mother's favorite, or at least one of her oft-cited, mottoes is "One can't pay enough for good help." This wasn't some perverse entitlement of the upper class. It was simply the dictum of a housework hater.

Indeed, my mother came from a long line of bookish women who hated pretty much every facet of domestic life. Cooking, laundry, mopping, washing dishes, tidying, and organizing (unless it was in relation to books) were not their bailiwick. Such busywork drained the mind and the soul; plus, they just weren't good at it. True, my nana did love needlepoint, and she always worked at embroidering lovely, functionless little pillows until in her later years her gnarled, arthritic fingers forbade it. But she was using the time spent in handiwork to think through Aeschylus, or what would have become of Christianity if the Greeks had gotten hold of it rather than the Romans. Ask my grandmother if you might have a little lunch, and what you got was a sliced apple matted with cinnamon powder, or maybe Campbell's beef consommé in a tempered glass mug ringed with the translucent flecks of whatever viscous pabulum it had last contained. She hired a cook to serve any group of more than four people. Nana's own mother, as well as her maiden aunts, had been the same way.

And so was my mother. She was the go-to person for a trenchant parsing of Jonson's "Cary Morrison Ode," but the kitchen and laundry basket rendered her powerless. She couldn't get things organized, or even tidy. Lurching stacks of books and papers were permanent architectural features of our dining room table; we ate in their shadow, in the small enclave described by their colonnade. The chieftain of the refrigerator was the old stoneware pitcher, whose primitive maw glistened with a mucilaginous brew of tap water and frozen orange juice concentrate. The bottoms of Pyrex baking dishes were mosaics in brown. That much went unnoticed. The rest had to be taken care of, so my mother always allotted a respectable portion of the household treasury to a cleaning crew. But such was her genuine detachment from the mores of housekeeping that she never realized that the crew was phoning it in. The top layer was attended to, but the by-products of human detritus remained in perpetuum. Had the cleaning crew been headed up by a stern Russian or Caribbean woman telegraphing her disapproval, my brother and I might have gotten the idea that someone was in charge. Even if we had felt a little embarrassed, we might have felt that even if there was no order in our home, Order itself did exist in Homes. As it was, I don't think either one of us gave it a second thought. Home was where Mom metabolized books and daytime television simultaneously.

In fact, it was also unclear to us who was in charge of the house. My mother's penchant for outsourcing domestic life had always called for a pageant of live-in babysitters. They lived in the garage out back, which my dad had refurbished into a one-bedroom apartment; they were there when we came home from school and, often, were the ones to put us to bed. Some were warm, attentive, and interesting. Marilyn, for example, was a fellow graduate student of Mom's, and she had a big gray cat named Luther, for Martin Luther, on whom she was writing her dissertation. I loved Marilyn; she was smart, snuggly, and reassuringly competent, and she called me her "little Susie" until she died when I was in my late twenties. Then there was Hilary, a choleric, overweight hippie who, when she wasn't getting mad at Ian and me, wrote very interesting, thoughtful poetry. She wore long, bustling patchwork skirts and asked her fiancé's daughter and me to be the "flower children" at her wedding, where we were supposed to leap around interpretively and fling flowers into the congregation (we were too embarrassed, so we ended up handing them out like canapés at a cocktail party).

But some of the babysitters were abusive. The most egregiously so, Bonnie, was also the prettiest and most charming: a raven-haired, ruby-lipped fairy-tale wicked stepmother. Bonnie would take us to parties at which she and her loser, handlebar-mustachioed boyfriend left us to range around bedraggled Berkeley communes while they smoked weed and watched porn with their creepy friends. She used to thrash Ian with a wire hairbrush, threaten me with worse when I impotently tried to intervene, and terrorize both of us to protect her secret activities. This went on for more than a year before I summoned the courage to out her. Though it was hardly a moral awakening: The reason I outed her was that she offered me 25 cents to babysit my brother and myself one night, and by that time, we were so inured to her cruelty that my response was not to tell her how scared or hurt we were by her proposition but to demand that she up the ante by 15 cents. When she balked, I groused about her scroogeyness to my mom. I was six years old; my brother was four. Although she canned Bonnie posthaste, my mother was mystified. Not only had it never occurred to her that a "professional" would behave in such a way, but she had never had the slightest indication that anything was off.

Off is, however, what things were, albeit not always in such harrowing ways—just in the weird ways particular to my family. Take weekly allowances. To earn theirs, my friends were charged with making their beds, setting the table, helping to weed the garden on the weekends. I had to memorize and recite poetry selected by my mother, as well as the entire lineage of the kings and queens of England. When friends did come over, my mother was not perkily interviewing them about what snacks they liked or what their favorite part of school was, but was propped up, robed and bespectacled, in her ancient four-poster bed—with *Hamlet,* various volumes of the *Oxford English Dictionary,* and the criticism of Harold Bloom layered in steppes. *Guiding Light* or *The Rockford Files* would be on in the background.

We were the weirdos. There was no point in trying to convey this to my mother. She was so consummately, unequivocally herself that she either would have said something like "Well, dear, that's just how our family has *always* been" or "The people you call 'weirdos' are usually the most interesting people," or she just wouldn't have known what I was talking about.

I would come to realize later in life that my mother belonged to a select tribe well known to English majors everywhere: the female English Renaissance scholar. At thirty, when I saw *W;t,* the play about a Donne scholar who is forced to see that everything is *not* a metaphor when she is struck with actual cancer, I did not see the fabulous, heartbreaking, childless character that my friends saw: I saw my mother. If you didn't see *W;t,* think back on your college days, recall that English lit class—Donne, Jonson, Herbert, Marvell—and if your professor was a woman, you have the gestalt of my mother in clear sight. The long line at the grocery store was not just a pain in the ass; it was a Chau*cer*ian pageant of *souls,* winding its way to re*past!* The fig salad you ordered at the yuppie bistro wasn't just skimpy on the figs. The salad was *chary* of figs, and actually *fig,* interestingly, was connected with the word "sycophant," which meant "showing the figs"—from the ancient Greek words "fig" and "to show"—and was used in ancient *Ath*ens to describe those who *snitched* on illegal fig expor*tat*ion to gain favor with high government officials, so perhaps *we* might appeal to the *chef* in sycophantic *terms* for a greater represen*tat*ion of figs in this otherwise most *elegant* of *salads.* Ta *da!*

No amount or type of life experience could knock the metaphor out of Mom. Every comment was elegantly footnoted, every moment linked to linguistic constructs or literary precepts, tropes, and conceits. In this, my mother was clearly not the typical Baby Boomer parent to my Gen-X child. She was not, like my friends' mothers, so preoccupied with finding herself that she either shunted off the kids' feelings with "I can't deal with this right now—there's too much on my plate!" or derailed a conversation into a monologue about what *she* was going through with her boyfriend right now.

But Mom was no less self-absorbed. Perhaps because nothing really happened *to* her but was, rather, strained through that scholarly, metaphysical membrane, my mother did not relate to direct experiences or feelings. She loved drama, loved talking, loved *discussing,* loved words. But she could not understand personal affect. All was simile, pumped up for maximum amplification. I was not actually struggling with a problem; I was *like* Jacob wrestling with God! I was not angry at people who made fun of my younger brother, Ian; I was *like* Antigone, defending my brother on pain of death. After my parents divorced, I was like Iphigenia, sacrificed for her father's ego; I was not a girl whose father had left. End scene. Whereas many X girls got the clear message that it was not they themselves but their Boomer mothers who were the protagonists in their lives, I understood that I was a dull facsimile of the tragic figures of ancient and Renaissance drama—and that my mother was the director. We were all understudies in someone else's theater.

Of course, as all readers discover sometime in adolescence, literature, poetry, and plays are the magical keys to the kingdom of human condition. We read literature to understand ourselves, to elevate the nobler ends of experience. By indoctrinating me in this habit, my mother gave me the skeleton key, for sure, but she imparted this gift to anyone smart enough to listen—most especially to her students. She was, is, a spellbinding teacher. If there was an award to be won, my mother won it; a grant to be awarded, my mother was awarded it; a teenage student in trouble, my mother was always the adult in whom she confided. Wherever she works, my mother is exalted.

But when you're the daughter, you just want your mom. You just want her to listen to you, to see you, to get what you mean. You want her to draw comparisons that help you understand her better, that help her understand you better—that help you understand yourself better. You don't want *Antigone*. Children, as it has been said, are literal thinkers.

My dad, when I was little, was as literal as a star. His delight in me was manifest. When I was born, he placed a tiny armadillo stuffie inside my bassinet and slept on the floor next to me. While my mother was writing and researching, my dad took me on climbs in the mountains, papoose-style. One of my favorite pictures is of me, at three months, and my dad nestled in an icy alpine cave, all bundled up. He's set up a tripod and is tenderly feeding me a bottle. There are other pictures, also rigged by tripod. There is one of Dad and me, just over a year old, taking my first step, on rugged terrain atop Mount Tamalpais in Marin County. There's Dad and me, age two, at nearby Stinson Beach, holding hands, his free hand pointing out at the gray, roiling Pacific, mine swinging a pink and yellow Easter basket. There's Dad and me on my first Halloween in conscious memory, age three.

The Halloween picture: Over the years, it has become an emblem. For one thing, Halloween was always Dad's favorite time of year; masks were his thing. As we grew older, Ian (my junior by two and a half years) and I made our own costumes, and Dad was always in on them. Ian went for enigmatic characters: a vampire Chinese ghost, the Masque of the Red Death. I favored inanimate objects: a postcard, a package of M&M's, a bunch of grapes. One time, Ian went as the mummy of some lesser-known pharaoh, and Dad built a sarcophagus apparatus laid over an oversized wheelbarrow. As Dad wheeled it around from door to door, Ian would push open the hinged cover, emerging with his track-or-treat bag in a ragged hand. That first Halloween, however, I dressed as Little Red Riding Hood, Dad as the wolf. Shortly after that photo was snapped, I became scared of his terrifying aspect. We shed the costumes and went as a little girl and her dad.

Certainly, in all these snapshots, one can observe early visual cues of those warring Gemini strains in Dad. The sharp-clawed, armored armadillo in the incarnation of a soft, cuddly stuffie. The cozy baby scene in the icy cave. The wild ocean and the Easter basket. But the one that emerges as something of a tarot card is the twin image of the adoring daughter and the uncomprehending prey, the Dad and the Wolf. Ultimately, as the hand played out over the course of my father's life, the beast would prevail. But such clues were not obvious at the time. Indeed, raging duality doesn't generally emerge as the central theme in a person's life and character unless it has the chance to develop in the proper environment. All villains follow the same path—they're just kicked in the right place at the right time. Which raises the question: If someone had been a little nicer to these guys, would that kick have had the force to hurl them into bona fide bad-die territory?

Mulling over the pivotal punt and its ensuing trajectory is the hobby of tragedy lovers like me everywhere. I'm not the first to have wondered, for example, if *Paradise Lost*'s Lucifer would have become Satan if he hadn't been unceremoniously evicted from Heaven. Had a little more patience and compassion been extended to him, maybe all that arrogance, anger, and self-pity would have blown over after a while, or at least have persisted as manageable character defects to be kept in check—not as the fiery pits of Hell. Had *King Lear*'s Gloucester degraded his illegitimate son even slightly less flagrantly, Edmund likely wouldn't have turned out to be such an evil punk. And knowing that she had such a volatile, immature son in Hamlet, couldn't Queen Gertrude have waited at least a year before marrying his *uncle*? I'm aware that deploying any one of these solutions would result in a mind-numbingly boring de-flation of drama—like trying to stage a Buddhist opera. But I've al-ways loved the villains; moreover, I've always wanted to *help* them. In my view, a little kindness, a little understanding is all it would have taken to turn these extraordinary characters around, to blunt the blows of outrageous fortune. As Lady Anne said to Richard III: "No beast so fierce but knows some touch of pity." But I came to this villain-rescuing way of thinking very early, literally before I can remember.

The watershed moment in my own paternal-filial dynamic was not documented in a picture, but rather played out in an event im-mortalized via family mythology. What actually happened seems to have been straightforwardly cute. Mom, Dad, and I had been driv-ing back late at night from a party, and the car broke down on the highway. Dad was swearing stormily, my mother devolved into her customary talky panic, and I, just over a year old, was asleep in the back. As the situation crescendoed, with Dad thrashing around for flares in the glove compartment, I suddenly chirped from my car seat, "Daddy-Doe, Daddy-Doe! Susie and Daddy-Doe!" My dad turned to his goofy-faced daughter, chortling in the dark. It was the first time I had uttered anything like a sentence, and it was a song. "Listen to her, Dugal!" my mother cried, thrilled. "Are you listening to your daughter?" He was. "Well, hello there, Suh-woo-zo!" he chuckled. Within fifteen minutes, he had cheered up, figured out how to fix the car, and was driving us home—with me singing my song all the way.

This incident, thereafter known as the "Susie and Daddy-Doe" song, became famous in our family and its circle of close friends. This inner coterie, it should be noted, were acquainted, to varying degrees, with Dad's good and evil inner twins. In very basic ways, they were explicit. On the one hand, Dad was, physically, one of those men you could identify from two blocks away as being Harvard Class of '60. He was, like all his ilk, an impeccable old-school preppy business dresser. Everything from his overcoat to suit to boxer shorts was Brooks Brothers. Tortoiseshell-framed glasses. Always. On the other hand, he was long on the loutish Libertarian bluster. You could always count on him to rail about downtown Berkeley's "lazy commie pinkos" and his character appraisal of Nixon as a "congenital thug" (ripped off from Hunter S. Thompson). He was open about his you're-goddamned-right-I-have-the-right-to-bear-arms membership in the National Rifle Association, though he was also actively involved in the Sierra Club and the Explorers Club; he worshipped his first-edition volumes of the naturalist writers John McPhee and Peter Matthiessen. Think Don Imus funneled into Dick Thornburgh.

And while Dad could, Imus-like, easily burn bridges with his guns-a-blarin' rhetoric, he was also deservedly known as a canny survivor. In his twenties, he had made the first solo ascent of the north face of the Gothics in the Adirondack Mountains, earning a place in the annals of American mountaineering; the route he pioneered is still known as "the Dugal." Throughout my childhood, Dad was always taking off to go on climbs involving backpacks full of neatly coiled ropes and clanking pitons. Once, when I was six and

Ian was four, Dad had gone on an epic climbing expedition in the Sierras with a buddy, and a freak blizzard buried the region where they had last been seen. My mother piled us into the station wagon, and we gunned it up to the base camp and found it teeming with rangers on walkie-talkies, TV news crews, and emergency rescue workers. My mother crumpled on the steering wheel. Ian wailed, clutching his favorite stuffie at the time, a Raggedy Andy that he had named, poignantly, "Doll Daddy." But there was no question in my mind that Dad was going to make it. When he and his pal were helicoptered to safety a few days later, emerging with rolls of spectacular film and having survived on a concoction he'd whipped up called "Mongolian milk" (powdered milk, snow, whiskey), Dad was fully intact, grubby and grinning like a teenage boy.

He was also notorious for being rib-cracklingly funny. Certainly grown-up men and women were always smiling broadly in his company—and, in short order, howling—but he was hilarious to my brother and me, too: a steady beat we could count on in the rhythm of everyday life. For example, Dad would be standing in the kitchen, his briefcase in one hand and a giant mug of coffee in the other, grumping in his Great Santini, ham-fisted way. But if he caught your eye, he might casually put the mug down on the counter, drop his briefcase on the floor, and spin into a graceful twirl and arabesque with his eyes reaching for heaven, then segue into a passionately furrowed Flamenco hand-clapping and foot-stomping piece. Then he would come to a complete stop on his tiptoes, set his heels down, and nonchalantly pick up the mug and the briefcase. When you laughed, he would bow and decorously intone, "And thus ends the recital of Julius Walrusso"—and leave for work.

But back in the evil-twin column, everyone who knew him also knew that Dad was just as likely to erupt into a molten rage as he was to crack a smile. He could be exquisitely vicious and foulmouthed, especially if he was on a binge. (Dad's alcoholism always colored everything he did, but when Ian and I were young, the tones were still pale; as he, and we, got older, they all but blacked out

everything about him.) But sometimes, the twin currents would converge like matter and antimatter—and then you were in for a treat.
There was the time, for example, when Dad went to the supermarket
to get some ice cream and became so outraged by the number of
flavors—as well as the amount and variety of nuts, candies, and
swirls bastardizing the pure, time-honored flavors—that he charged
into the manager's office and ranted that "we" didn't want "this ob-
scene array of choices, this New York super fudge almond chunk
nougat swirly stripe bullshit"; he, frankly, found it "ostentatious and
aggressive." He didn't know what was "going on here," but he simply wanted to put the manager on notice that "we" just wanted
"Butter Brickle! Plain and simple!" "We" didn't want all this "goddamned frippery." "We" never asked for it, and "we" wanted "no
part" of it. When my dad relayed this story to me after the fact, I remained silent, while he sat there fuming at the memory of it. After a
few moments, I ventured, "You know, Dad, I actually really like all
that stuff—especially the kind with the peanut butter cups." My dad
balked. "*Really?*" He considered this, then nodded. "Well, perhaps I
owe that hardworking citizen an apology." I howled. He scratched
his chin.

The trick was knowing what would tip the balance from bad to
good—and, really, that's what made the "Susie and Daddy-Doe"
story so telling to people close to us. Especially to my mother. In her
rendition of that night, it was pitch-black outside, there were no
other cars on the road, and Dad had been so violently enraged about
the car that he was a hair's breadth away from a tantrum that she
was not sure she could control. She was scared. But then, she said, I
had somehow known *precisely* what to say and *how* to say it so that
calm, arrowlike, would penetrate my father's *roiling* soul. People
would nod knowingly, sometimes reaching out to pat my mother's
hand and looking at me as though I knew a secret. "That little girl
loved her daddy," she would whisper, tearily.

My dad, a self-declared enemy of emotional hyperbole, would
never enter into such discourse. Indeed, he loathed metaphor and

what he referred to as "endless discussion"; he liked chutzpah, guts, gonzoism. But his concession to the veracity of Susie and Daddy-Doe came shortly thereafter in the invention of a bedtime story he called "The Adventures of Beverly Noodle." A charming and agile strand of pasta, Beverly Noodle was forever finding herself in tough spots—an icy crevasse, a den of criminals—and, with the help of her kind-hearted, well-adjusted friend and assistant, Sebastian the Donkey, she was always able to rally her singular combination of wit and grit to figure her way out.

To the extent that Dad would countenance metaphor, there was no question whom he intended these characters to represent. Dad, who extended the Beverly allegory by referring to himself in our workaday lives as the "noodler-in-chief," was always figuring things out, and I, often tapped in the "noodling" process—Sebastian the Donkey—was henceforth dubbed "the deputy noodler." I loved being the deputy noodler. The job involved everything from figuring out how to pack a hiking backpack for maximum efficiency to determining which annuals to plant where in the garden based on color and height to more esoteric conundrums like figuring out what quarks were. Although Dad spent his career as the marketing director for various high-level investment funds, his métiers, other than ice climbing, were photography, painting, gardening, astronomy, and geology, and those passions often converged on expeditions, even everyday ones.

"Now, think about *this,* if you would," he once posited to me on a run to the local plant nursery when I was around ten. "They've just discovered a new particle, and the scientists describe it as 'the absence of nothing'—now, what in hell does *that* mean?" I considered this and then said that the absence of nothing seemed like it had to be everything. My Dad slammed his hand on the steering wheel. "That's *exactly* it!" he hooted. "I've been thinking about it all week, and *you got it!*" He laughed and shook his head. "Tell you what, there, little darlin'," he said, grinning at me in the rearview mirror.

"What we got us here is not just one drop-dead beautiful *and* one funny-as-hell cookie—we got us one *smart* cookie."

Noodler-in-chief and deputy noodler. As I approached school age, I evinced a more demonstrable sense of grit, the trait my dad most admired. In part because one of his heroes was the explorer John Wesley Powell, who famously navigated and mapped the Grand Canyon for the geographical survey of the U.S. government *without an arm* (it had been blown off during action in the Civil War), my dad relentlessly marketed the idea that grit is more important than talent. He would take my brother and me on camping trips in the Sierras, sometimes compelling us to hike—as seven- and five-year-olds—upward of ten miles a day. Ian would flop poutily on a rock and refuse to budge. I'd keep my head down and press on. You always felt incredibly nauseated in the mornings because of the altitude, and while my brother would, understandably, complain, I made it a point to suck it up. "Tough as nails, Suze," he'd declare with gruff pride.

But the ultimate honor was the Arctic Trip. As reward for my proven determination to tough it out, Dad made me a special promise when I was around eight: When I turned twelve, he and I would take a trip up to Ellesmere Island. The northernmost island in the Canadian Archipelago, Ellesmere Island appealed to my dad as an ice climber; the place is virtually all icy mountains, and practically nothing grows there. But he was also drawn to what he imagined would be the singularity of the void. "There's just *nothing* up there," he'd marvel. The plan was that it would be a "troopers only" expedition, just the two of us: hard-core camping, climbing, and canoeing. We would not bathe; we would eat nothing but Ding-Dongs and Kool-Aid. "I bet you and I will be the only two crazy honkies up there, Suze-o."

Did I really have a well of native grit, or did my love for my dad—and fear of losing my deputy noodler status—compel me to dig one? I don't know. I know that I couldn't wait for that trip. Could. Not.

Wait. I could not believe that my notoriously gonzo, smart, funny, ice-climbing dad had selected *me* to take on the most serious expedition he had ever conceived. It meant, in my mind, that I not only had the right stuff; I must have *more* of the right stuff than anyone else he knew. He invited *me*. My father, who was so extraordinary, saw something extraordinary in *me*. Not only that, but he saw that we shared the *same* extraordinary traits. Dad and *me*.

Now, in one sense, it was true: We were both pretty curious (dilettantish), determined (obdurate), and fond of a good laugh. Whether such traits are in fact extraordinary is arguable, and in any case that wasn't the issue for me as a kid. Simply, my father saw what I was; my mom just couldn't. Though I know that she loved me, her way of looking at the world was so fundamentally different from mine that we were rarely able to pull off a successful noncognitive transmission. Also, perhaps because I was a girl, as well the namesake of six generations of esteemed Susan Gregorys, she became increasingly distraught as she perceived that with every year, I was failing more and more to fall in line with "the women of our family." Classic bluestocking ladies, the matriarchs in my lineage conformed not to the Hestia or Demeter archetype but to the Emily Dickinson profile, preferring to choose their own society—a society most often restricted to books and a select group of people who liked to talk about books. That I liked a lot of other things besides books confounded my mother. When I was young, this frustrated her to the extent that her normally weird but loving nicknames for me—"pickle-ator-pumpkin" and "magic muffin"—were often supplanted with "miserable failure," among others. I now know that she didn't mean it, but at the time, such characterizations made me feel very bad about who, in fact, I was.

My dad, however, gave genuine thought to my ideas and observations, literally snorted milk out his nose laughing at my jokes, took actual pleasure in my company. I sensed that my dad didn't love me just because, as my father, he kind of had to; he actually *liked* me. Even as a little kid, I was aware that he did not react this way to everyone. A telltale polite, resigned smile crept across his lips whenever he was faced with an encounter it became clear he would have to endure, or if someone made a joke he did not find funny. Ian, for example, was often forced to regard Dad's portrait in blasé tolerance. It was heartbreaking: Ian adored Dad the way a puppy loves his boy. He bounded around, frantically working every angle he could think of to get Dad's attention, to mimic Dad's humor. But, as often happens when people get increasingly anxious to please, Ian would overdo it, and that, for Dad—master of the fun and the easy—was an instant deal-breaker. Dad would simply give Ian the smile and move on to the next activity. Once, after a particularly furious bid to get Dad to laugh, Ian exploded. "How come every time *Suze* says something, you think it's so funny, but every time *I* say something, you don't?" Dad calmly scooped ice cream into a bowl. "Well, Ian," he said, "*vive la différence.*"

It wasn't fair, Dad's treatment of Ian, and I didn't get anything out of feeling favored. Then again, Ian was, without question, Mom's darling, and I was inextricably bound to Dad, largely because I needed his protection. Around the time I turned ten, our household became tense, forbidding. My mother had started teaching at Stanford, and the commute from Berkeley was a killer. She wanted to move to Palo Alto. Dad did not. That was all my brother and I know, factually speaking, but it was clear that Dad was grumbly. A lot more grumbly. His grit and gonzoism began to morph into fierce rigidity and unaccountable black moods. But so far as his interactions with me were concerned, Dad was still noodler-in-chief. Whenever my frenzied, stressed mother was screaming at me after dinner, Dad would simply instruct me to get into the car: "Sit tight, Suze." I'll never know what he said to her, but he would burst out of the house, slam the car door, and head for the Berkeley Hills. We'd get out at the summit and observe constellations. "Look at that, old pal," he said, pointing a thick index finger upward. "That star there, at the tip of Orion, is a *whole other galaxy.*"

It was only within the past several years, after a lot of researching and reporting I did for professional journalistic purposes (and therapy for my addled psyche) that I had one of those revelations that instantly illuminate all the murky primal feelings. It emerged from reading I did—with my first baby snuggled next to me on the messy bed—about studies on infant attachment. It's old news to anyone who has read anything at all about children's development in the past twenty years or so, but to me, it was flat-out jaw-dropping material. Babies are actually born *needing* to bond to someone—who knew? Renowned pediatrician Penelope Leach cites studies that show that in order to thrive, babies need to attach to a primary caregiver within the first six months of life. Without healthy attachment to such a person, a baby can develop what is called "reactive attachment disorder," a mental health condition most often seen in cases in which babies or very young children have passed through a succession of different foster care situations, lived in orphanages, or endured prolonged hospitalization; have experienced the sudden death of a parent, or divorce; or have had multiple caregivers, parents or regular caregivers with mental illness or drug and alcohol problems, or mothers with postpartum depression. According to the Mayo Clinic, children with this disorder exhibit one of two types of behavior: "inhibited" ("shunning relationships to virtually everyone") and "disinhibited" (attempting to "form inappropriate and shallow attachments to virtually everyone, including strangers"). According to Mayo, such children "can't give or receive affection."

The good news is that, so far as a baby is concerned, it doesn't particularly matter if the candidate for attachment is an aunt, an older brother, a grandparent, or a nurse at an orphanage. The only thing that matters is that the person lovingly and consistently attends to the baby's needs: reading the baby's cues, responding to them, and, most important, perhaps, taking genuine delight in the tiny creature. In return, that person becomes, to the baby, "mother."

As my life has lurched forward, my appreciation of this concept has been as helpful as it has been poignant. It illuminates a previously invisible framework for so many of my decisions and neuroses. It helps to explain why I married the man I married; a big part of why I never, ever would have imagined in a billion years that I would get divorced. I think it also in some way explains why I, like a great many of my Generation X compadres, practiced—and still do—a modified form of "attachment parenting." And it may also explain why my marriage fell apart a little more than a year after my father died. Because here's the thing: Until I was ten, my dad *was* my mother.

But when I was eleven, everything changed. After living in Stanford for a year, we moved to the Main Line suburbs of Philadelphia, a blue-blooded territory comprising old estates, debutantes, elite prep schools, and country clubs that excluded minority members. My father had been offered a job with a fast-growing financial services company, and to keep the family together, my mother agreed to the move, giving up her position at Stanford. She hated it. We hated it. The weather was awful, the neighbors were austere and remote—so were the kids, none of whom seemed to ride bikes after school but who were occupied with sports like lacrosse and field hockey. Our house was so big that it took two furnaces to heat, and there was an entire floor that we never used. (After John Lennon was killed, I assumed proprietorship, dedicating the bedrooms to theme shrines devoted to each individual Beatle.) My brother's room was in a completely separate wing from mine, and it was freezing. He was always getting sick. I felt scared for him, being alone there. Sometimes I would come to check on him on especially cold nights and find him shivering under his polyester-filled comforter, clinging to his elephant stuffie, Harold. I couldn't understand why our parents didn't do something.

There was a lot that we didn't understand.

Although of course she must have, it seemed our mother never got out of bed the first year we lived back east. Being in bed has always been among her favorite occupations, but this was different. She wasn't reading metaphysical poetry while half-watching *Perry Mason*. She was always sleeping, always in the same nightgown. "Just get up and come outside with us," we would urge nervously. "Oh, okay—in a bit," she would croak. But she never did.

Dad hated it, too. He had always been the most popular guy on the block, the first to break the awkward first moments of a cocktail party with some fantastic story or outlandish observation that yielded laughter and looseness. But his charms were lost on the patriarchs of Main Line Philadelphia. "Goddamned stuffed shirts," he would growl. "These guys are living off trust funds set up for them in the last century—not one of them has worked an honest day in his life." More and more, Dad would come home after we were asleep and leave for work before we woke up. He drank more and more. On the nights he was at home, he would fall asleep in front of the TV, his fist still clenching a tumbler of scotch.

But after the first year, Mom got out of bed and got a job as head of the English department at a posh private school. Dad all but vanished, away on business trips. The last time he materialized in the context of our family was for what would turn out to be our last vacation together. We drove up to the Pocono Mountains, where friends had lent us the use of their cabin. Dad brought no climbing gear. "These aren't mountains," he snarled. "They're just shitty hills." He did, however, bring his telescope; we planned to look at the stars that night. When we arrived, the sun was merciless. Mom went indoors to unpack groceries and read, and Dad sat on the unsheltered patio with a tumbler of scotch, squinting out into the lawn and the field of tall, dead grass that lay beyond it. Ian and I had decided to make a bushwhacking trek into the grass, having been instructed by our mother to pull up our socks to avoid "penetration by ticks." As we were crossing the yard en route to the field, Ian stopped suddenly. "Look!" he cried. I stopped and scanned. Everywhere, it seemed, there were bunnies, nibbling on stalks of grass and dandelions. Bunnies—they were so little! Their tiny upside-down-Y-shaped mouths quivered with agonizing cuteness, their hops like miniature lopes. "Look, Dad, look!" we hooted. "Bunnies!" He smiled faintly. "Look at that," he said. Ian and I bent down and watched them earnestly, as if in that instant we had become charged with their care. After five minutes or so, we heard the first shriek.

It was unworldly, like the scream of the ghost of a murdered child. Ian and I looked at each other, panicked. What had happened? Then there was another shriek, and another. We screamed when we saw them: snakes. Tethers of black snakes were coasting through the grass. There were so many. Ian and I ran wildly, bawling, trying to rescue the bunnies, but our attempts scared them, forcing them into the tall grass, where they were killed. We screamed for our father. Dad ambled onto the lawn and stooped to pick up a twitching bunny, attacked but left behind in the melee. He placed it carefully in the backseat of the car, where it writhed in the sunlight. Ian and I sobbed. My dad folded his arms and looked at the little thing with a sad frown. We tried to feed it some grass, some water. After a few hours, it seemed revived, and Dad told us to set it loose. We did. Within minutes of its disappearing into the tall grass, we heard its shriek.

A thunderstorm rolled in by dinnertime. No stars. That night, I am told, I sleepwalked. I flew from bedroom door to bedroom door, begging at each one: "Let me out! Let me out!"

Room. Poems. Gash. Sleepwalking. Stars. Ice.

Dad.

One way in which my personal themes converge with my generation's is in the primacy of *Star Wars*, which contains the archetypes of home, wounds, stars, ice, and fathers—dark and light. Since having my own children, I've thought a lot about *Star Wars*. It came out in 1977, and it is still a huge, huge deal to X. People my age take their *preschoolers* to see it—*three*-year-olds. Why are people my age so attached, in such a primal way, to it? Generation X people, including me, rarely hesitate when asked to name the defining cultural and developmental turning point of their childhood. Like you have to ask: *Star Wars,* man! It was *huge.* One day, you were a total babe in the woods, a Piagetian changeling. After *Star Wars,* you entered Life. It's not just that *Star Wars* changed the toy industry, play patterns, the movie and fast-food industries. It was the galvanizing experience of our generation in the way that the anti–Vietnam War movement was for Baby Boomers. But why? Why is it *still* such a huge deal? How did *Star Wars* become a major milestone in our children's lives, too?*

I've come to think that the answer may be something like this: If our parents' divorces were the wars we endured in private, *Star Wars* was the war that unified us culturally. Prompt a grown Gen-X guy, and it's rarely long before he launches into a play-by-play recon of action scenes in *Star Wars* as though he were an actual veteran. Gen-X women look to Princess Leia as a Rosie the Riveter icon. But I believe that the narrative themes of *Star Wars* were what so deeply resonated with us. Luke Skywalker may have been conceived of by his creators as a prewar Clark Kent–type farm boy, but to 1970s children, he was one of us: the ultimate latchkey kid. He was on his own a lot; he had to handle a bunch of adult responsibilities so the household could function. Then: *kaboom!* His family was destroyed, charred beyond recognition. The mother and father figures were recast instantly, violently. The Oedipal mother figure was now a smart career woman on a serious mission, with no time for crybabies, who looked hot in a Linda Ronstadt kind of way (with the glistening, wine-colored lip gloss). Han Solo was Mom's cool boyfriend, with his fast, junky-looking bachelor ride; Darth Vader, the terrifying half-human, half-robot Dad, hell-bent on either getting you on his side or destroying you. *Star Wars* might be the epic custody battle of all time.

---

* On Inauguration Day 2009, *The New York Times* ran a front-page story featuring a photograph of just-about-to-be President Barack Obama holding a beaming ten-month-old infant wearing a seventies-style rainbow T-shirt. The baby's name was Jedi Scott. Jedi.

In our generation's own, real-life *Star Wars*, though, the burning down of the Skywalker family farm was the Important Family Announcement. Ask anyone whose parents divorced, and they'll cite the Important Family Announcement as being one of the most traumatic experiences of their childhoods. The Important Family Announcement was, essentially, the Genesis story for Generation X's narcissistic wound. It's like this: The family, pre-divorce, was its own sort of Eden—an imperfect and quotidian one, but an Eden nevertheless in its gestalt of permanence and predictability. And then came the Important Family Announcement. It began with the parents sitting the kids down in the den or family room. The dad, hollowed-out and remote—with the mom nearby, red-eyed and quivering—explained that "your mother and I do not love each other anymore" and "can't live together as a family," but that "we love you kids" and "feel that we're all going to be happier in the long run."

The eerie formality, compounded with the stunning disclosure that one's parents not only had separate lives but were empowered to dissolve the indissoluble, made the Important Family Announcement hallucinatory. Parents' postmortem to themselves, their friends, that "the kids seemed to take it well" was delusional. The kids were in a fugue state. For years.

With the nucleus of the family, once stable and prosaic, blown apart, the landscape became postapocalyptic. The father, heretofore a somewhat remote disciplinarian with whom you could occasionally roughhouse and be gross, was now trying to annihilate the mother with legal proceedings and character slander and was installed in some interim bachelor pad, absently spoiling the children with toys, junk food, and movies on the weekends. The mother, after about a year in depression during which she leaned terrifyingly on the children for emotional support, "reinvented" herself on a full-time career track, attending aerobics classes and dating a string of divorcés. Darth Vader, Princess Leia at war. There was no safe place to land.

My high school was littered with such sad-eyed, bruised nomads.

There were perennial migrant flocks of latchkey kids in the suburbs, wandering from used record shops, to behind the train station to get high, to the parks they used to play in as children; they trudged back and forth from their mothers' houses during the week to their fathers' apartments on the weekends. In one of the most egregious cases, the divorced parents of a teenage boy I knew installed him in his own apartment because neither wanted him at home post–Important Family Announcement. Naturally, we all descended on his place after school—sometimes during school—to drink and do drugs. He was always wasted no matter what time we arrived. A few years ago, a friend told me she had learned that he had drunk himself to death by age thirty. A very close friend of mine, at fifteen, managed both of her parents as they collapsed under the weight of their respective mental breakdowns in the wake of the Important Family Announcement, each of them clawing at her constantly; in the meantime, she did her best to keep her two younger siblings together. Now in her forties, she lives alone, ready to answer triage calls from her family.

In my own family's case, the Important Family Announcement landed on my little brother's birthday. His tenth birthday. At this point, Ian and I did not grasp that our parents were estranged, much less getting divorced. We knew that things seemed terrible in a general sense and that Dad had been "on a business trip" when our mother was away in England. On this day, what we understood was that, for some reason we did not understand, our father was not there on Ian's birthday. Where was Dad? Mom didn't know, but she reassured us that Dad was certainly on his way. Morning gave way to noon, then afternoon. My brother, my mother, and I wandered in and out of the house, sometimes intersecting. At some point in midafternoon, my wanderings had taken me into the kitchen, where I had just opened the freezer to reach for a Swanson's chicken pot pie. Suddenly, Dad was there.

"Howdy, old pal," he said. He was wearing a jeans jacket. A

jeans jacket. He clapped me on the shoulder like a man, strode into the pantry, and poured himself a scotch.

"Well, Suze," he said, "as you've probably surmised, your mother and I are splitting." He oriented his empty tumbler on the rippled tile counter, sauntered around the kitchen table, and stopped at the window to regard the vegetable garden he had planted. "The basic idea is this: I've reached a point in my life where I realize that I've done nothing for *me,* and I'll be goddamned if I'm not going to do it." He went on to explain that he was sick and tired of doing things for "the kids" and "your goddamned mother"—it was time for *Dugal* to do what *Dugal* wanted to do. Life here was just plain shitty. Why should he have to put up with "all kinds of ingratitude" as his reward for working "for those cocksuckers"? He was *done.* He poured himself another scotch and spat out details about the unsatisfactory complexion of my mother's and his sexual relations. He then announced that he had met "just a terrific woman" who he was sure I'd think was terrific, too, and he leaned back and ruminated rosily about the woman's virtues and the quality of the connection that he had with her. He put down his drink.

"So, that's the story, old Suze," he said, thumping me on the back. "It'll take some getting used to, but you'll be fine. You're tough." And he left.

Recently, my brother and I were on the phone, talking about Ian's newly born second child and my newly born third. We started talking about Dad, and that moment came up. "Yeah," he said, in a prolonged drawl. "Did you know that Dad never even said hello to me that day—my *birthday?*" I had not. I don't know which was worse.

Many of the years following the Important Family Announcement are best left forgotten. Which is why it is impossible to do so. Our mother was feral in her grief, which often found an outlet in cursing me and cosseting Ian. My defensive maneuver was either to fight back or to flee in operatic style; Ian's was to withdraw, either in paralysis or in fury. Ian and I rarely saw our father after that; were it not for my parents' divorce agreement specifying four visits annually, we probably would not have seen him at all. When we visited him in Massachusetts, he was either not there or passed out. His wife, a clenching fury, never seemed to sleep. Terrible things happened.

Ian tried. There was still the idea of mountain climbing, and every so often, it would seem to take form. Once, when Ian was in high school, Dad told him he would take him on a weekend expedition in the Adirondacks. With the climbing and camping gear packed up in the trunk, Dad drove them to a motel in the foothills. He left as soon as they opened the door to the room and returned with a case of vodka. Ian watched television while Dad drank. "When are we going to go climbing, Dad?" Ian would ask. Dad didn't respond. They never left the motel room. After two days of Dad drinking straight from the bottle and Ian watching TV, Dad drove Ian back to boarding school.

When I was a teenager, I received a bunch of giant boxes in the mail. They were filled with polar camping equipment: sleeping bags, parkas, boots, pitons, crampons. There was a note: "Get ready.— Dad." The Ellesmere Island trip—it was *on*. Noodle-in-chief and deputy noodler. Then, without a word, he took his wife's daughter. He sent me a hand-carved Inuit statue of a howling golem: half man, half monster.

"There was something terrible in me sometimes at night I could see it grinning at me I could see it through them grinning at me through their faces it's gone now and I'm sick," said Caddy Compson in *The Sound and the Fury*. In my senior year of high school, I was put in a psychiatric ward. After a battery of tests and medications produced no diagnosable results, my mother pled with the head psychiatrist to offer some pathology that would supply explanation. "Your daughter," he said, "is suffering from deep terror."

After my parents divorced, one of the sad, weird things that happened was that I completely lost my bearings in the night sky. As a kid, I was the undisputed Pleiades and Little Dipper finder. I can still find them, but it takes me forever. I can't see Orion unless it is pointed out to me.

———◆›×‹◆———

TWO

KISS THEM FOR ME:
FIRST LOVE

One of the books in the *Star Wars* prequel series is called *Rogue Planet*. The plot runs something like this: The rogue, or orphan, planet where the action takes place is actually sentient and can travel anywhere it wants to in space. There is a vibe of Neoplatonism on the planet, because its earliest inhabitants believed that the Force is inherently light; ergo, there is no Dark Side, but only twisted, selfish practitioners who manipulate the Force for ill—a philosophy known in *Star Wars* terms as "Potentium." In the story, Obi-Wan Kenobi and the future Darth Vader, Anakin Skywalker, go to the rogue planet to track down a missing Jedi knight who turns out, in spite of her adherence to Potentium, to sacrifice herself to save the "good" guys. But ultimately the bad guys attack the rogue planet anyway, which consequently hoofs it to what the *Star Wars* lexicon calls "Unknown Regions"—parts of space that are unnavigable to all but those who are supersensitive to the Force.

Although the narrative, like many of the *Star Wars* prequels, is pretty thin and crappy, I find the themes presented in *Rogue Planet* irresistibly suited to X metaphors. There is something very moving to me about the way in which the *Star Wars* ontology recasts an orphan planet as a rogue entity that is not only the master of its own mind and destiny, but also maintains a very clear-eyed, karmic perspective on all the hyperbolic goings-on in its warring universe. And when it all gets too hostile and confusing, the rogue planet retreats to uncharted territory. There is something fundamentally Xish about this rogue planet's configuration—or at least the way in which X has often been depicted, and has depicted itself, in popular culture.

Think, for example, of the 1980s hard-core punk song "Institutionalized" by Suicidal Tendencies (immortalized via the soundtrack of the 1984 X movie classic *Repo Man*), in which the protagonist recounts that his efforts to sit quietly and meditate on his decisions and goals are relentlessly interrupted by shrill and ultimately malevolent authority figures who misinterpret his introspective affect as dangerously unhinged and corral him into a psych ward, over his objection that all he "wanted was a Pepsi," rendering the song itself his retreat. Fast-forward to Eminem's X anthem and the title of his 2008 autobiography, *The Way I Am,* partly a diatribe against the opposing sociological characterizations of him as either a bigoted hatemonger (conservative blabbermouth Bill O'Reilly declared that Eminem was "as harmful to America as any al-Qaeda fanatic") or the messenger of a lost generation (as a research fellow at Stanford's Hoover Institution wrote in an article entitled "Eminem Is Right," "If yesterday's rock was the music of abandon, today's is that of abandon*ment*") and partly a Zen-like acquiescence to it: "I am whatever you say I am." Potentium, in a nutshell.

But really, take your pick. From the Circle Jerks to *The Breakfast Club* and everything in between, virtually every X hero is drawn as a maverick who sees through society's machinations and therefore re-fuses to conform: We never *wanted* to be in your orbit anyway, ass-holes! Like the Star Wars rogue planet, X makes a virtue of rejection. And actually we can be pretty funny about it. Indeed, some of the most gut-splitting exchanges I've ever had have been series of one-upmanship about bad incidents from parental-abandonment, split-family, latchkey childhood. If you're not of this generation, it sounds sick. It *is* a little sick. But it's funny. One friend told me that once, at a boozy seventies family party, she and the other parents' kids were jumping on a bed when she catapulted off and suffered a bleeding head wound. She ran to her mother, who, with one hand swirling a glass of Chablis, reached into her purse with the free one, yanked out a Maxi pad, stuck it on her daughter's head, and said: "You're fine—now, go back and play!" Another friend (call her Emily) recounts stories of her single mother doing all manner of inappropriate things in front of her children: going out on dates in miniskirts and stilet-tos; drinking an entire bottle of wine herself as she recalled all the good times she'd had with her many boyfriends in high school; flirt-ing with Emily's own high-school boyfriends. Whenever Emily and her siblings bring these stories up with their mother now, she will sigh, shake her head, and simply say: "Well, that was a very dif-ficult period for me." This begs for sketch comedy. "Hey, Mom—remember the time you smoked crack, put on pasties, and did a lap dance for my tenth-grade AP chemistry teacher on parents' night?" "Yes, well, honey, that was a very difficult period for me."

But here's a poignant twist on the rogue planet metaphor: It turns out that rogue planets are not, in actual life, just *Star Wars* meta-phors. Not only are they real, but their actual cosmic fate is pretty sad. Recently, I stumbled across a documentary on a science channel about this relatively "new" type of planet. When the first of these celestial bodies were detected in the early part of the twenty-first century, the narrator informed us, astronomers didn't know how to categorize them. On the one hand, they certainly looked, and had formed, like regular planets. But on the other hand, they were missing the crucial element: a sun. Evidently, gravitational force had violently expelled them early on from their solar systems, pushing them away at fifty thousand miles per hour. After that, the planets were rendered nomads. I was so struck by this that I went to the astronomy news site Space.com and read this passage: "In a mere decade, the home star shrinks to a point of light, eventually indistinguishable from other stars of the sky," the article read. "This is an orphan world, wandering without destination in the numbing, frigid desert of deep space." There are a lot of orphan planets; one astronomer at U.C. Santa Cruz reported that he wouldn't be surprised if 50 percent of planets were "rogue." It is also possible that, as I have read, beneath their frozen crusts, these planets conceal life at their cores.

An orphan world, wandering without destination in the numbing, frigid desert of deep space—one of perhaps *half* of all planets in the known universe—that even after years of solar neglect may still harbor a beating heart? You can't expect the *Star Wars* generation, more than half of whom grew up in the culture of the nest-expelling divorces of the seventies and eighties—and who are now today's child-attached alterna-dads and moms—to pass up that metaphor. Moreover, however handily neat and potentially tacky that parallel may be, it poses too many rich, allegorical questions that bore into the murky core of our relationships with our parents, our spouses, our children—indeed, into the core of our very genesis.

We can be as maverick, caustic, and snickery as we please about our own origins; when you quietly pause to peer in at those formative experiences, they are often—like the real rogue planets'—just plain grim. Who remembers riding in the way-back of the station wagon with the dog and no seat belt? Probably most of us. Shoot, I remember riding in the *front* seat with no seat belt, as an eight-year-old (and my head cracking the windshield when my dad abruptly slammed on the brakes to avoid running a red light in front of a cop). Who remembers the days before all these fussy "child-proofing" safety measures were de rigueur? I have giant scars from third-degree burns running up and down my arms marking indelible hieroglyphics from that laissez-faire period of American child rearing. Like many American children of the 1970s, my friends and I were left in the back of the car during grocery runs to the Safeway, and were consequently exposed to our fair share of leering, masturbating perverts in adjacent vehicles. Disgusting, but probably not unusual. At twelve, just after my parents had separated, I spent the night at a friend's house in which no parents were present and the older brother was compulsively watching porn on a giant TV in the family room, and that night he came on to me aggressively, with such animated images as backdrop. Again, not uncommon. A similar situation emerged on a semi-regular basis at the parentless home of another friend, minus the porn. Same deal.

Same deal for a lot of us. Consider this random sampling, chosen with no special deliberation but from the top of my head. A friend I'll call Jeremy, who grew up on the West Coast, was regularly compelled, at six years of age, to comfort his single mother as she lay crying on the bathroom floor playing "Send in the Clowns" over and over again; weekend visits with his heavy-drinking father often amounted to trips to the homes of unstable girlfriends and their roving wolf-pack children, who introduced him prematurely to drugs and sex. According to another friend, "Carrie," her elementary school years in Wisconsin were spent watching TV after school with her brothers while her father smoked pot and "worked" at his desk. Her parents were always throwing bacchanalian parties, occasionally of the "key party" variety depicted in *The Ice Storm*, Rick Moody's odyssey of the byways of suburban marital degeneracy in the 1970s. My friend "Julie," who grew up in Texas, grew up in a house littered with her father's print pornography collection, his carelessly degrading comments, and her mother's nervous silence. One of my oldest friends, "Jessica," and her siblings had to themselves an entire floor of their childhood home outside Philadelphia, where they spent much of their time smoking pot, drinking siphoned-off liquor from their parents' stash, and isolating in adolescent angst, with rare check-ins from their parents, who entertained frequently in the lower living quarters. (At twelve, I smoked my first cigarette and got drunk for the first time on that floor.) Jessica's sister, now a mother of three, had this comment about the one-story ranch in which she's raising her own family now: "My kids are not going to be on their own floor, crying alone."

On their own floor, crying alone. An orphan world, wandering without destination in the numbing, frigid desert of deep space. Unknown Regions. The locus of X's narcissistic wound is sure to be found in these vicinities.

As a parent now, it frankly blows me away to ruminate on the way so many of us lived as kids. Holy shit. How were we supposed to approach dating and relationships—much less marriage—after having hatched from such solitary confinement? Can the orphan planet ever latch on to a new star? It certainly can't do it by merely flirting with the outer orbit of whatever solar system it happens to be hurtling past along its solitary, pointless trajectory. In physics, it turns out that for the orphan, theoretically, to have a shot at the sure embrace of a sun, it would have to be hurled, and pulled, into it by massive gravitational power. All in or not at all.

In the thousands of conversations I have had with hundreds upon hundreds of Xers who came from divorced households of the 1970s and '80s, very few of them honestly say they actually ever dated. Had random, lost sex? Yes. Chucked themselves headlong at relationships, whether or not they were involved with the right person? Definitely. All in or not at all.

The peak age in girls' psychosexual efflorescence is thirteen, and for me, turning thirteen converged with my dad's official leaving and, within a few months of that, with my mother's regularly depositing me after school at the home of family friends. The parents were often not present, but their almost-twenty-year-old son invariably was. This young man, whom I'll call Pete, was instantly cast in my mind as the older brother figure, the prospective new star. No dad? There was Pete. I liked Pete. Pete liked me. He was demonstrably tickled by my snark. Like every northeastern prep school ninth grader, I toted around a dog-eared and heavily underlined copy of *The Catcher in the Rye,* so I was delighted by Pete's Holden Caulfield gestalt. We had actual smart teenage conversations, which I had never had before, having only recently become a teenager myself.

Plus, Pete knew about real music. He had been in a band of the King Crimson/Traffic/Gentle Giant variety, and his room was meticulously patchworked from ceiling to floor with posters featuring the album cover artwork of bands known to music-heads as *real* musicians. I became Pete's student in colloquia on the primacy of guitarists like Jimmy Page, Randy Rhoads, Edgar Winter, and Al Di Meola; on stylus care and the key differences between various makes of subwoofer; on how to parse liner notes for salient information. Pete's parents let him smoke in his room, and since the door was always shut, I learned to roll my own Drum cigarettes and blow smoke rings nonchalantly, perched on my knees on his tapestry-covered floor in my school uniform's short navy blue kilt and gray knee socks. He took me to parties with his college-aged friends who went to cool, smart schools like Oberlin and Wesleyan. He looked out for me.

In this regard, I might have been like any girl with a big brother. But I was not, as it turned out. Although I had cast him as big brother, Pete had seen himself in a different role. The night he disclosed this by leaning into me on my twin bed while our parents were engaged in a dinner party downstairs, he grinned, kissing me on the mouth: "You knew this was going to happen." I had not known. He was so much older—I had not known at all. As he pressed me into my rainbow comforter, I started to laugh. "You kill me!" I said, parroting Holden Caulfield. "You kill me!"

The Greeks knew what happens when fatherless daughters are allowed to wander unattended to pick flowers in open fields. The girl is swallowed up by Hades, eats the pomegranate seeds (the food of the dead), and returns at least seeming like a woman, certainly changed and rootless. Something dark and familiar rushed through my gut the first time I read these lines in Louise Glück's poem "Persephone the Wanderer": "Is she / at home nowhere? Is she / a born wanderer?"

I didn't know where to go, what to do—not then, not in the weeks and the months that followed, and since it was already done anyway, it didn't seem to make much difference that it continued. My mother, alternately frantic about keeping her job and swooning with grief over my father's leaving us, did not really register that I essentially vanished. I started dropping out of the things that I had been good at doing, like field hockey and theater; my formerly large circle of friends narrowed to about two. And I smoked. A lot. I started smoking at thirteen, up to almost a pack a day by the time I was fifteen; within the year, I had done most the drugs of the era. In short order, I seemed to be someone who knew a lot. My mother, I think, noted a newly forged steeliness, but I was simply, in her mind, "advanced," as I was, in her mind, in all things. And Pete's parents, after all, were doing her a tremendous favor.

It would later surface that Pete's parents had known that their son had feelings for me, and in hindsight, this may have been their reason for helping my mother with the after-school arrangement. They were worried sick about Pete because he, as it turned out, had suffered a great deal. Three years before, he had been involved in a car accident in which a girl he loved was killed. Psychotherapy and major surgery had propped him up in the physical world, but he had not shown signs of emotional recuperation. They wanted their son to be happy. So when Pete wanted me to sleep over, they acquiesced, waving me in the direction of the guest room. My mother never said no. I would lie in the guest room bed expecting Pete to come for me, and he always did. That winter I was taken on a family vacation to Mexico, where fancy friends of Pete's parents from Houston joined us. While I sat by the pool in a bikini that Pete had bought me at the gift shop, the woman stared at me from under her broad-brimmed hat and whispered to her husband. Pete knocked on the door of my hotel room every night.

Not long after Mexico, I was snowed in at Pete's house. I woke up in the middle of the night with a hot, intense pain on my left side, just below my abdomen. Worried that it was appendicitis, Pete roused his father, who was a doctor—a psychiatrist. Dr. Lisle, whose birthday happened to be the same as my dad's, smiled awkwardly and asked me to lift my shirt slightly so that he could press on the region in question. "You are sure that the pain is on the left?" he asked. Yes, I was. He nodded and excused himself to phone a colleague. Meanwhile, Mrs. Lisle emerged, arms folded in bathrobe, looking at Pete, whose eyes were pinned on me, hand on my thigh. When he returned, Dr. Lisle reported that I did not have appendicitis; the appendix is on the right. More likely, I was experiencing *mittelschmerz*. "What in God's name is *that*?" barked Mrs. Lisle. The doctor ignored her. "I have to ask you, Susie," he said, an uncomfortable smile anticipating the predicate. "How long have you been menstruating?" I flushed. More than a year, I said. "What does that mean, Evan?" said Mrs. Lisle. *Mittelschmerz,* said Dr. Lisle, is a pain that some women experience when the egg breaks free of the fallopian tube: I was ovulating. Everyone looked at one another. "Ah," said Mrs. Lisle finally.

That fall, I went to boarding school.

In the interim, like so many girls in the early eighties, I went from schoolgirl to ravaged little punk essentially overnight. A lot of suburban girls adopted the punk uniform for the fun of wearing tarty Halloween costumes all year round: heavy makeup, ripped fishnet stockings, teensy tartan kilts. But I didn't want to look like Billy Idol arm candy; I wanted to crush and be crushed in the mosh pit. I loved the angry, boyish brouhaha of the D.C. hard-core punk scene. I chopped off my hair and dyed it black, white, purple, blue. I wore oversized shirts and boots. I haunted used record shops, combing through hand-printed records and zines. But I didn't want to be, or look like, a boy, or even wholly punk. I liked looking like an androgynous waif, inhabiting a generative style netherworld of my own design. Annie Lennox looked too much like a drag queen for my asceticism (plus, the Eurythmics were too bubble gummy for me); Laurie Anderson, though unimpeachably cool, was too pretty. My esthetic eidolons formed a transgendered pantheon: David Bowie; Patti Smith; Joan of Arc; Anne Carlisle in the classic New Wave indie movie *Liquid Sky;* Sid Vicious; Paul Westerberg; Ian McCulloch; Iggy Pop; David Byrne. When I saw Bergman's *Fanny and Alexander* in 1982 and saw the kindly, cruel, and utterly asexual character Ismael, I breathed: "Yes."

Looking back on that stage, it's obvious that there was more to it than just liking the look. The concomitant experiences of having been dumped by the roadside by my dad and having my incipient sexual self pried open by an older guy left me so exposed and raw that I had no time to manufacture any normal boundaries with the male counterpart in general—or to develop my own sexual personhood. I was dependent and fearful, and at the same time full of fury and resentment. I was, at some level, trying to erase my manifest sexuality. I wasn't going to be Lolita again. In fact, my gestalt—pre-Pete—had been almost identical to the voiceless Lolita's (the eponymous novel having always been, shockingly, my favorite not at all for its content but for my slavish admiration of its style; after I had my daughters, I couldn't even look at it). For one thing, I had been at twelve and thirteen that selfsame snarky, fashiony pubescent girl whom puerile men and bitter women wrongly deem precocious and wise beyond her years. For another, my story followed the same crudely drawn lines. The parents are gone; the immature father figure steps in; the girl is idolized even as she is privately exploited; somehow the whole thing is made into a sickening love story. Something in me snaps when I hear people appraise my own girls as being "so grown up." Let's get this straight: No one is wise beyond her years. More likely, she is coping with a situation from which she cannot escape by grasping at adult props she thinks will help her survive. I remember the first time I read Humbert Humbert's poem, and it still reverberates in black spots:

Where are you hiding, Dolores Haze?
Why are you hiding, darling?
(I talk in a daze, I walk in a maze
I cannot get out, said the starling).

But, of course, *Lolita* is a love story. All stories of incest are love stories, however grotesquely distorted, and *Lolita* is fundamentally a story about father-daughter incest. As I see it, a collapsed Cliffs Notes summary of incest literature and *Lolita* might say something like this: Not only does the orphaned pubescent girl need a father, but her hormones are raging; she cannot help but respond to this perverse sexual relationship. In the ideal world, a girl of this age has a father figure who adores and admires her and provides her with appropriate boundaries. Because the father is her primary source of male emotional support, she can explore her budding sexuality with someone her own age without risk of opening herself up to catastrophic exploitation. Since she does not overly depend on her fellow explorer to protect her ego and psyche, there is an innocence about sex, an almost purely physical sense of wonder and discovery—an advanced game of doctor. This was not the story for Lolita and me.

It is the conflation of all the above that makes incest, or relationships with all the underpinnings of it, so complicated, particularly if it happens at the onset of puberty. In thinking about all the thousands of conversations I've had on this topic with friends my age, I have begun to mull over a murky, troubling thought. Where our primary, spousal relationships are concerned, I wonder if a great many of us fall on this spectrum of the incest relationship paradigm. In other words, our relationships with our husbands or partners are filling in for a father-daughter relationship we never had.

I recetly reread a landmark study that seems to speak directly to this point. The study—conducted in the early 1970s by the eminent University of Virginia psychologist E. Mavis Hetherington—followed the lives of three groups of adolescent girls into adulthood: those from intact families with an involved father; those who had lost their fathers to death; and those whose fathers were absent because of divorce. Broadly speaking, what Hetherington found was that the girls from the first group had, not surprisingly, the healthiest interactions with boys and men. They tended to have positive perceptions of their dads, and their responses to boys and men were generally natural, confident, and grounded in their own terms. Girls whose fathers had died were more likely to have an idealized image of their dads; they tended to avoid boys and men and were shy and self-conscious in their company. But the girls whose fathers were absent because of divorce had a very different response. Although they had negative perceptions of fathers, these girls were more likely to flirt, to be promiscuous, and to get married earlier—to inappropriate men—than their peers. They tended to overdepend on men for their sense of self, security, and sexuality even as they had trouble forming long-term attachments to them.

That third group makes me think about *Fast Times at Ridgemont High* and the Jennifer Jason Leigh character, Stacy. In one of the final scenes, Stacy and Linda (Phoebe Cates) are chatting at the diner where they both waitress:

STACY: You know, Linda. I've finally figured it out. It's not sex I want. Anyone can have sex.
LINDA: What do you want?
STACY: I want romance.
LINDA: Romance in Ridgemont? We don't even get cable TV.

The scene is even better in context, which is that Stacy had begun the academic year receiving extremely practical, almost clinical, sex counsel from Linda (we never see Stacy's—or anyone's—parents throughout the entire movie; the kids are always shown on their own, at work, at home, at school). By this time, Stacy has had sex twice, with two different guys; had an abortion, for which the guy (Mike Damone, the skeevy scalper) neither showed nor paid; and finally fallen for the guy she'd liked all along, the lovely, albeit nebbishy, and smitten Mark Ratner ("the Rat"). In this scene, Stacy has just finished her freshman year. She is fifteen—and she has already had her middle-age "Aha!" moment.

I totally got this scene. I, for one, was already into my second major relationship by the time I was fifteen. Most X teenagers got it, too, which is why the movie is now considered our classic. For us, it seems the path to dating, sex, and love was utterly retrogressive. Indeed, our approach was categorically different from those of our immediate predecessors. In the 1950s and early '60s, courtship was reinforced by a cultural environment of Eisenhower-era optimism, friendliness, and civility: Boy meets girl; boy invites girl to soda shop; boy gives girl varsity letter jacket to wear; boy and girl "go steady"—a term that beautifully encapsulates the quaint, reassuring socioemotional gestalt of the era's budding romantic relationships. "Going steady" gave way to "free love" by the late 1960s and '70s, the ecstatic abandon that emerged, thanks to Baby Boomers' having been reared by Dr. Spock–trained parents. It just isn't possible to act out with such blissful abandon unless you're fundamentally secure. Neurotic people, however, lack the emotional foundation for such freedom. Neurotic people are guarded, calculating, political, scared. Hello, friends! That was us. The mores of teenage neurosis form the very premise of *Fast Times at Ridgemont High*, and, for that matter, of most of the greatest hits of 1980s popular culture. Indeed, a thumbnail review of the top movies, songs, and literature of the day—*The Breakfast Club; Heathers; Less Than Zero;* big hair versus shoe-gazing bands—reveals that the top romantic feelings were sullenness, sarcasm, revenge, fear, and vulnerability. Notorious for the Whartonesque social hierarchies established in high schools and malls, we approached one another with the presumption of rejection, competition, and power struggles.

All that edgy posturing was the stuff of our crunchy crusts, but what about our gooey centers—particularly, what about the gooey centers of girls like Stacy? Was she looking for a father figure in the skeevy scalper, Mike Damone? Was it Damone's ethical obligation to refuse her, on the grounds that he was older and occupied a position of relative power? What was Stacy really saying to the Phoebe Cates character by reporting—after her wild, troubled run with a string of coercive older guys—that she now wanted "romance," not "sex"? Was she saying that she wanted the kind of healthy, nonsexual father-daughter romance with the sweet, nonthreatening Mark Ratner—"Rat"—that she should have been having with her actual father? In the absence of her actual father, what should she have done? That is, what is the best course for those of us in Hetherington's third group? Are we doomed to quasi-incestuous relations with our mates—with or without sex? What is the safest route? The healthiest route? Even if you've spent years in therapy, how do you really sort all this out?

Not to say that it's any easier for guys. Studies from Harvard, Penn State, and an array of other major research universities have been reporting since the 1960s that boys who grow up without a regular, involved dad tend to engage in "overcompensatory masculine behaviors" or "protest masculinity." The basic takeaway from this research is that these boys are so dominated by their mothers, and female authority in general (grandmothers, teachers, babysitters, and so on), that as they grow into men, they need to divorce themselves from it by engaging in behaviors that academics label thus: "rejection of authority, particularly when it is imposed by adult females"; "exaggerated masculinity"; "a relatively exploitative attitude toward females, with sexual contact appearing as important as conquest and as a means of validating masculinity." Basically, they're assholes.

Everyone who grew up with a single mom knows these guys: You either went out with them, you had them as brothers, or, if you're a guy, you *were* them. Much of the only truly original music to have been produced in the 1980s—early rap, hip-hop, hard-core punk— was predicated on such "protest masculinity." Friends of mine from relatively well-adjusted families of origin (or those in which the father was still totally involved, a relative rarity when we grew up) were outraged back in the day by rappers' gross misogynistic repertoire, especially by Eminem's psycho-Oedipal brand of it. There is no question that it's awful from a social and civic point of view, and I share the outrage (especially when I think of my own daughters). But there is part of me that on a primal, genetic level feels a sisterly simpatico with these guys, particularly with Eminem. Out-of-control single mom, no father to speak of, the mother's and children's financial collapse and degradation following divorce, the kids belonging to neither this social world nor that one but floating in a purgatorial netherworld of their own, then, after all that, the girlfriend whom he adores fails him, too? Even if this isn't exactly what happened, it's obvious from his body of work that this is pretty much what he feels happened—and as such, there's a part of me that totally gets it. My take on it is that Eminem is mainly mad at his mom and his ex-wife for not being a better mother and wife and that there is some random, boyish spillover from all that abandonment.

This is not to say that there are not undoubtedly sociopathic freaks who really do hate girls and women; there are also probably those who are confused and unhinged enough to say terrible things just because everyone else does or because they feel that they have to show off. Those people are dangerous. But the standard-issue "protest masculinity" guys? In my mind, they're all to some extent like my brother, my stepbrothers, and a great many of my guy friends (and to some extent fatherless guys throughout history, like Caesar Augustus, Hamlet, Bill Clinton). There's just no way around it, as anyone with firsthand experience knows: It's tough sledding for boys growing up with a single mom.

Ian was definitely on this continuum. My mother—in part, I think, because she came from a family that had been dominated by generations of intense, supersmart women—seemed to think that my brother needed "special help" because he was more "fragile" than I was, when, in my view, he was just a regular boy, and a really smart boy at that. With the paternal toughening, man-upping influence deleted from his sphere, Ian was alternately coddled and shamefully pitied, leaned on and dissected. I, for one, found this intolerable, enraging. Sometimes, I'd yell at my mother to stop treating Ian like a pathetic moron whose every minor achievement was cause for pompom waving, and I'd yell at Ian to stop acting like such a pussy. Other times, I'd attempt to explain to my mother calmly (and, undoubtedly, condescendingly) that her inappropriate nursing of Ian was actually deflating his self-esteem and capacity for genuine competence. I'd give Ian a St. Crispin's Day pep talk, barking at him that he was as sharp as all get-out and that he needed to stop defaulting to Mom's characterizations of him to justify his self-pity and inertia— he was better than that. Then I'd yell at both of them for their creepy codependence and feel sorry for myself for not having a parent with whom I could share my own weird codependence.

Unsurprisingly, this triangulation did not do much for Ian (nor any of us). He resented me for being, by ludicrous default, the "nonpathetic" child, so when I got into trouble, which was incessantly, Ian enjoyed assuming the posture of a powerfully annoying Dickensian Tiny Tim, sorrowfully tucking in under Mom's wing and sticking his tongue out at me. But every so often, Ian would erupt into a surprise fit of primal male rage. Coming from a massive teenage male of six foot four, these bouts resulted in overturned tables and book ripping. I never blamed him for these. He was, after all, a *guy*. Moreover, he was a guy sandwiched between two warring maternal figures, each of whom believed she knew what was best for him. What guy *wouldn't* lose it and devolve into chest-beating tantrums?

To this day, Ian alternates between indulging women's troubles and his own fears, and getting grouchy when a woman close to him

(Mom, me, his wife) asks him to do something that might in some unconscious way call his manhood into question (do the dishes, for example). But Ian is awesome, and in spite of it all, he married a fantastic woman; I am close to both of them, and I am rooting for their union. And although Ian got mad at me for getting the lion's share of the attention (even though it was almost all negative), flaunted his Little Lord Fauntleroy status, and definitely freaked whenever I got bossy with him, he never got mad at me for pushing him. He still doesn't. Ian needed a father, and that's what fathers do. They push you. My thinking is this: When you're the son, mothers want you to do stuff for *them*; fathers want you to do stuff for *yourself*. Ergo, misplaced rage betides the man who was raised by the single mom without paternal presence.

Take my friend "Mark," for example. Mark was the oldest of three boys whose father left them for a woman with her own children; the father never looked back. So Mark grew up under the alternately asphyxiating and abject wing of his single mother, who constantly implored him to take care of man-of-the-house things for her: mowing the lawn, fixing the sink, patching the roof. While he was occupied at those jobs, she lavished attention on him, but she basically ignored him when he wasn't, instead lavishing the attention on the younger brothers—which made him mad, though he wasn't exactly aware that he was mad at the time. Mark subsequently married, and had children with, a woman with whom he had virtually no sexual connection but who asked him to do a lot of man-of-the-house jobs. After he ultimately divorced her in a surprise fit of rage, Mark took a job that worked him fourteen hours a day, six days a week. Although he believes that he would like to be in a relationship, he now gets mad anytime someone he is dating requests anything of him. So he works like a dog and spends all of his free time with his kids.

Another friend, "Scott," one of four boys, was the son his single mother felt was most like her and could understand her better than anyone else. Scott grew up listening to his mother's troubles, trying to help her sort through them, and co-parenting his brothers. When his mother remarried when he was in his late teens, Scott was demoted to being his mother's backup sounding board, the man she called on when she felt that her husband couldn't understand her. Scott spent a good part of his thirties with a narcissistic older woman with a young son from a previous marriage, which had ended in an ugly divorce and an absent father. Scott devoted himself to listening to his girlfriend's troubles, fending off her ex-husband's dunderheadedness, and co-parenting her boy. In a surprise fit of rage, Scott broke up with her and now longs for a wife and family, dating one woman after another, breaking up with the older ones when they become too needy and with the younger ones when their immaturity is laid bare. He stays in touch with his ex-girlfriend's son.

I could go on. But in essence, the results of my armchair field study: The single-mom-and-son dynamic breeds emotional incest. I know there are exceptions, and all blessings and admiration are most deservedly theirs. But in my experience and in a great many others', these relationships with their sons generally end up codependent—particularly if money is tight, which, statistically, it almost always is for single mothers (a chief risk factor for women falling under the poverty line is divorce). Such circumstances are outrageously stressful on single mothers with little outside help. But unless these women are highly self-aware and can avail themselves of appropriate emotional support, they often lean on their sons. Which often leads to filial dysfunction with a distinctly incestuous undertone.

No mother but the truly sick wants to do this. But it's pretty much a gimme that the son is essentially forced to be the husband: a tragic setup on the Greek order. No matter how hard he tries, the son is doomed to feel like an impotent loser. He knows he is powerless to alleviate the mother's financial and emotional stress, and even if he is too young to know about the mechanics of sex, he has the sense that he isn't man enough to be a useful partner. But the mother still exerts such emotional pressure, however obliquely, and the son feels every square millimeter of it. Often this powder keg is set off when the son is dumped unceremoniously if a boyfriend or stepfather steps in. Now he feels betrayed *and* unmanned, his hurt made worse by the boyfriend's unspoken but clear resentment and competition with the son. The question is, what was anyone expecting *other* than "protest masculinity"?

Obviously, this mother-son configuration is at least as old as Oedipus. But because more boys were raised by single mothers in the 1980s than ever before in U.S. history—because there were more divorces—such Oedipal meshugas came to define a respectable margin of X's generational anthropology, not only of human relations, but also of the culture. While predecessors like Philip Roth, Charles Bukowski, and Henry Miller might have shared similar angry-young-man DNA, Xers were distinguished for their lacerating self-awareness and shame. Think Bret Easton Ellis, Marshall Mathers, Kurt Cobain, Rick Moody, Douglas Coupland, almost all the eighties punk-rock band leaders you can name, and one of my favorite personal cases in point, the poet and Sarah Lawrence College professor Jeffrey McDaniel.

I met Jeff in the wake of both our parents' divorces. Because of late (or no) child-support payments circa 1984, my mother, younger brother, and I had moved to a Soviet bloc style, ill-maintained apartment building in suburban Philadelphia inhabited by elderly people and divorcées. Jeff moved in with his dad, who lived down the hall from us, apparently in the wake of some bad goings-down with his mother, who lived in the city. Jeff attended the prep school where my mother was head of the English department (probably one of the reasons Jeff and I, wisely, never really became friends). But I always half-tracked him throughout high school because whenever I walked past his apartment, he was listening to the same music I was. Plus, I liked his whole affect: sneery, punky, writerly, clearly exhibiting protest masculinity. I'd pass Jeff with one of his legion of girlfriends, moodily trudging the streets of Bryn Mawr with his earring and combat boots.

A lifetime later, when I was groping through the bleakest period of my divorce, I found a book of grown-up Jeff's poetry next to Pablo Neruda's at Barnes & Noble. And what do you know? His work nails the kind of narcissistic wound exacted from that whole Generation X son–single mom thing, in a wry, self-lacerating, and street-y way. Consider this poem, "The Jeffrey McDaniel Show":

I walk into a candlelit room.
All the women I've ever dated
are passing around the love poems
I gave them, and guess what?
It's the same poem—My sweet
[Put Your Name Here] if I was God
I'd make flowers smell like the back
of your neck, trees with trunks
as soft as your thighs. When we kiss
I feel like a cheerleader being crushed
to death by a giant pom-pom. Then Alex
Trebek appears. A game of Ex-
Girlfriend Jeopardy ensues.
All the categories about me.
"I'll take emotional baggage, Alex,
for twenty." "Jeffrey's mother
spanked him with this blunt object
so hard, he couldn't look in a mirror
for a week." "What's a wire hairbrush?"
"Correct, you control the board."
"Bedroom Arrogance, for thirty."
"The most narcissistic thing Jeffrey
has ever said while making love."
"What is . . . ?" If you hold me real tight,
you can feel the centrifugal force
of the world revolving around me.

And as if to offer a close parenthesis, consider this pithy stanza from another of his poems, "The Jerk":

> You're not really my new girlfriend,
> just another flop sequel of the first one,
> who was based on the true story of my mother.

And there you have it: the ipso facto Oedipal Gen-X man. I have, we all have, known so many of them that describing their basic gestalt is almost like writing a horoscope profile. They are furious and self-incriminating, charming and resourceful. They can seem like consummate rescuers until their scabs are ripped off by women who they feel are manipulating them or treating their efforts with indifference, mockery, or egregious clinginess. Then, look out. They can become Madonna-whore-complex-struggling, redemption-seeking humiliation junkies. Personal observation and experience suggest, however, that this kind of guy comes into his own in a relationship with someone who genuinely values his competence and helpfulness, as well as his masculine virtues in their various forms. My feeling is that guys like this *need* to feel needed and appreciated, which is why they often make especially doting fathers. This is a man I understand. Why? I had the same mom. I had the same dad, too: the absent one.

This meant, for me and people like me, that the mate selection process was, depending on how you looked at it, either so complicated as to be statistically impossible or really quite simple: Get sucked into someone's orbit.

The first love of my life was a guy I'll call Jai—the yoga name that his parents cursed him with, and they couldn't have chosen a worse guy for it. Jai looked like a lusty cross between David Bowie and Jack Nicholson, and he could not have been less calm and centered. In fact, when I saw my first Eminem "Slim Shady" video years later,

I was full of delighted recognition: Jai! Jai was gorgeous and feral and funny and smart and angry. He raced bikes with sustained, intense fury and had the most Adonis-like body of any guy I have ever known before or since. Everyone wanted Jai: teachers, girls, guys, little brothers, mothers. But the best part about Jai was that he was devoted to one thing: me!

We met at boarding school, one of those third-tier sorts for kids who had been kicked out of someplace better. Students were housed in the upper floors of the school's main building, divided into "Girls' End" and "Boys' End." Jai and I didn't so much know each other as eye each other, and since Jai was eyed by everyone, that didn't mean much to me. I was known primarily as the punky girl whose off-campus boyfriend (Pete) was always sneaking her off to the city. Then, one early winter morning, on the students' return from breakfast, each of the girls of Girls' End discovered a note in her mailbox. Each communiqué was profoundly and explicitly insulting, a brutal inventory of that young woman's flaws in the estimation of the authors. My note, however, was not. It was rapturous, worshipful, panting. And it was, as one shrill know-it-all pointed out loudly, written in Jai's handwriting.

I don't have to tell you that this was—and depending on the day, just about remains—the best fucking moment of my life. To be sure, it was great that he was hot and kooky and the main event. But that wasn't what made this event so exquisitely transcendent to me. For a fifteen-year-old girl with an acute case of unrequited Elektra complex, it was that I was The One. He saw me, chose me, conspired with his fellows, bankrupted his reputation—risked school ousting—for me. For *me*. Reader, he could have had teeth growing out of his ears. I was his.

In the end, we got kicked out of that boarding school. Jai had to move back to D.C. with his dad; I returned to my mother's place outside Philadelphia. Still, we stayed together for nearly three years, and we saw each other every weekend. *Every weekend.* By that time I was sixteen years old; Jai was eighteen. He dropped out of high school, took the GED, and became a TV producer; I went to a local public high school, where I was an exotic boarding school expellee and angry writer-in-residence (a status that, to my ambivalence, isolated me from the main population). But though we lived hundreds of miles apart, there was never any question in our minds that we would stay together. Jai either rode his motorcycle up I-95 to me, or I dashed out of Friday's last class and ran directly to Amtrak, where I would plunk down in the smoking car and produce essays, short stories, songs, poems, and sketches of Jai in various guises. My mother wouldn't let us sleep in the same bed, but Jai's father was deeply moved by our guileless devotion to each other (probably because he was Russian) and gave us our own room in his apartment.

It never fails to elicit jaw-dropping responses when I tell people that our parents did not quibble with this arrangement. I suppose it's partially that, first of all, the divorced parents were just too taxed by this time to stand firm on anything. But they must also have had the sense that Jai and I did actually love and buoy each other in ways that they couldn't or didn't. Easier to countenance a radically unorthodox relationship between a pair of delinquent teenagers than to undertake the alternative: Deal with us.

But our epic teenage love story finally ended when the long-distance commute began to get to me. I promised Jai that we'd get back together once I graduated from high school. He snapped and launched an array of distressing tactics: phone calls from window ledges; middle-of-the-night high-speed trips from D.C. to my mom's apartment, culminating in Jai's bellowing beneath my window like Stanley Kowalski; anguished, angry letters. Ian was heartbroken; he adored Jai. What was I doing? I was wretched and torn. On the one hand, Jai was my psychic twin, My Guy. On the other hand, I was seventeen. I was going to a sis-boom-bah public high school, complete with freaks, geeks, jocks—the whole *Pretty in Pink* ecology. Everyone was dating, going to parties, being *kids*. I observed the scene as if it were unfolding in a different dimension. I inhabited Unknown Regions. Still, maybe I could try to be normal. Was I such a ruined mutant that I couldn't fit into a traditionally functioning solar system, too?

It would become clear that the answer was a resounding yes. For years, I regretted letting go of Jai. I would never understand someone else as well, or be as well understood, again—without risking more than I was willing to risk via any audition process. In other words, I could not date.

I do not understand dating at all, and for that reason, I have never done it. Yet were you and I to meet, this would probably not be your impression. It's not that I don't like hanging out with guys. I have always loved hanging out with guys; I love the whole guy talk shtick. It's not that I don't think sex is good; I think it is quite good. Moreover, although I don't really see it this way because it sounds bad and inappropriate to me, I am told that I am a catholic flirt: I flirt with young and old men and women, babies, dogs, birds, everybody (except cats). My point is that, to the world, I apparently present as someone who would date, and maybe date a lot. No. No freaking way. The mere idea that I would agree to go to dinner or drinks with someone, with the naked subtext of "Does either of us want to sleep with the other?" running like a prurient news crawl underneath the veneer of conversation, is so fantastically upsetting and alien to me that it actually makes me sick to my stomach. I know that this makes me nuts. Yet there it is. My feeling is: Why are we even watching this movie if we're not getting married? (I would do very well in the Orthodox community, my Orthodox friends tell me. Then I show them my tattoos. Okay, maybe not so much, Susie.)

My version of dating was: Watch, sniff, wait, and then signal. There was nothing civilized about it. Indeed, my process unconsciously mimicked animal mating strategies because I was, after all, a wounded animal looking for protection. It wasn't until after I had already been with my husband for well over a decade that I began to understand the ways in which my incipient sexual identity had been hobbled by the circumstances of my father's leaving and my conjoining with Pete—which had, unconsciously, compelled me to set up job candidates for the position of safeguarding my gnarled-up little psyche. And let me tell you, that position was a serious business. I now see that there was a pattern to the way my courtship strategy worked. I was never a note passer or a rank-and-file coquette, though I have always, as mentioned, been at ease with, and taken genuine pleasure in, guyish company. Again, I also seemed a lot older than I was, not surprising since I had been doing older things for a few years already. I had advanced tastes. I seemed, in short, like someone who knew a lot about a lot. But of course I didn't. Just because you've had a lot of experiences doesn't necessarily mean you're wise. It makes me think of the fallacy of that hackneyed Nietzsche saw: "That which does not kill us makes us stronger." This is something that people seem to say when they either have not yet been through an experience that actually did come close to killing them, or they can't make sense of life's horrors. I can definitely understand the impulse, but still, it has always struck me as utter horseshit.*

At any rate, my experiences hadn't killed me, but from Jai on, whenever the vibe smacked of dating—in any given school, college, workplace, or regular social situation—I would hang back and disappear out the back door. To me, this was basic self-protection: entering into anything resembling an emotionally intimate scenario would render me utterly defenseless, vulnerable, childlike. I couldn't do this with anyone casually, so I'd chat, joke caustically, have a giggle, and exit. But to others, I was later told, such behavior bespoke an attractive unavailability. Who knew? It never fails to amaze me

---

* Interestingly, it turns out that it *is* utter horseshit. In a 2009 report published in the journal *Nature Neuroscience,* researchers at McGill University found that child abuse can so traumatize developing brains that it actually mutates DNA by modifying the gene NR3C1, which is responsible for modulating stress response. These genetic changes suggest that abuse survivors may have neurological trouble turning off the stress response, resulting in a constant stressful state, leading to future problems with depression, anxiety, and possibly even suicide. So, that which doesn't kill us does *not* make us stronger. It just doesn't kill us. (Plus, seriously, Nietzsche himself knew better: He had a series of nervous breakdowns and had to move in with his sister.)

that one's deep and abiding neuroses can, when masked, seem like something marvelous to the outside world.

But now, as I reflect on my behavior, I wonder: *Was* I, on some subterranean level, trying to string guys along? Maybe I did unconsciously intend to cultivate an air of mystery, knowing that only the most determined—and therefore potentially the most worthy—would answer the call. If so, it certainly wouldn't make me unique. It's a typical female sexual strategy across species. The female displays herself at the appropriate time, lets the guys show off and duke it out, and then chooses the mate who has demonstrated the most impressive quotient of power and success. But measures of power and success are, obviously, subjective, and to me, the qualifiers were not how good-looking you were, how rich you were, if you were the quarterback on the football team, if you were funnier and smarter than everyone else—or even if you had *all* these things going for you. For me, and for girls like me, you did not have to be perfect in and of yourself. You had to be perfect for *me*.

The order was this: Be my father, best friend, and love machine all in one person. Make me the absolute center of the universe, the most adored, the most desired, the most fascinating creature ever to have inhaled a single breath on earth. Annul the past; you have no past. Your life began when you first glimpsed me. In return, you are Everything.

This is self-centered, unfair, implausible, unhealthy. Indeed, such consuming needs are the ugly psychic offspring of the narcissistically wounded, so the psychiatric literature tells us. Denied attention early in life, we inhale it as adults. Indeed, we see the objects of our affection as very young children see their parents and want their parents to see them: *As it was in the beginning, is now, and ever shall be, world without end.*

That's how we feel, even if we're loath to admit it or even countenance the thought of it. Even as a teenager, I hated that in myself. But forcing all my eggs into one hapless little basket seemed like the only option, or at least *my* only option. To suggest to me that I should just go out with people "for fun" would have been like telling an alcoholic to have just "a drink." The alcoholic does not want *a* drink. The alcoholic wants thirty drinks, and because of this, she knows it is better to have no drinks at all rather than to attempt, and fail at, one or two (or three or six). So it was with me and guys. Better to be completely abstinent than to date casually.

So, as eager as I was to be assigned a walk-on part in it, the whole Brat Pack ethos remained utterly foreign to me. The adolescent romance was not, for me, about secretly making out behind the gym with the misunderstood, angry punk-rocker guy and hiding it from your cheerleader friends. Neither was it about being the school slut going to the homecoming dance with the sweet nebbish from AP chemistry. There was only one thing, in capital letters: LOVE. Love was *everything*. It wasn't just a Springsteen-born yearning to know love is wild and real (though that isn't bad). Love had to be more than that. Love had to make a permanent dent in that wireframe grid of the universe. "I am thinking of aurochs and angels, the secret of durable pigments, prophetic sonnets, the refuge of art. And this is the only immortality you and I may share, my Lolita." *Exactly.*

Thus courtship became highly distorted. I felt too internally wounded to risk playing the field to find the right person. I had to develop wolflike attention and the discipline of a sniper. It would be easy to be distracted. Certain people I liked a lot; they were funny, smart, cute, interested in the things I was. But if I could not smell on them that particular pheromone that signaled to me that they had similar genes, then considering anything even resembling an intimate connection with them was a nonchoice. Suffice it to say, there were few choices.

For a period of time in high school, I attempted to anesthetize myself under the numbing mask of cocaine and sundry other drugs. It more or less did the trick in that regard. It did not, unsurprisingly, in others. When I found myself, at nineteen, living on a crack corner in North Philadelphia with a boyfriend (the first post-Jai) who had honestly tried to do his best by me but with whom I was nonetheless headed down a terrible path, I left and hurled myself at work. I got a job as a reporter at a construction newspaper in Philadelphia. I was very aware of how alone I was. At this point, my mother and I were estranged; my rebellious behavior with that boyfriend had compelled her, probably prudently, to let me go. I'm not sure that my father knew or thought about where I was. I remember walking alone across an empty lot in North Philadelphia that winter, wondering: Who will identify my body if I die?

I got an apartment share, had a smattering of brief and sordid dalliances (which couldn't count as dates but rather hair-tearingly shameful drunken hookups), but mainly I worked and worked and worked. I enrolled at Temple University, for which I paid myself; although it had been specified in my parents' divorce agreement that my father would pay college tuition, he had reneged on the contract. I saved up enough money to sue him, but we were able to settle out of court. I had had no contact with him for more than a year, but I called to tell him that I had applied and gotten in to Columbia. He was silent on the other end of the line. "Good going, Suze," he finally said, quietly. "You haven't done it with any help from me, that's for damn sure." I asked him if he would like to help now. He told me to tell his secretary where to send the check; then he hung up.

I worked hard. I transferred to Columbia and was on the dean's list every semester, and I was proud. I did not hang out with any particular group. All the psychic horsepower I had expended in my teens into thrusting myself into someone's orbit found a new course in grinding intellectual toil and massive output. I was a machine. I felt durable, self-sufficient. I took nine classes in my final semester of college; all A's. My mother and I began talking on the phone, and by and by we came to enjoy each other. After a period of stealth dating, she got engaged to Joseph, whom I liked on the spot and trusted shortly thereafter—unprecedented for me. It was almost surreal how good he was: brilliant, prudent, ethical, kind. I was so happy for my mother; I was overjoyed for Ian and me. (I still am, twenty years later.) But my father continued to rip me up.

My father came to visit me once while I was at Columbia, during one of his stints of trying to get sober. He came uptown to my dorm, having made a presentation on Wall Street. When the elevator doors opened, he was unimpeachably dressed, as usual. He stepped out with his briefcase in one hand, cradling on his shoulder with the other a giant cardboard box of O'Doul's nonalcoholic beer. "Howdy, there, Suze," he puffed, and blew past me into the hallway. He kicked open the door to my room, plunked the box down, sat on the end of my bed, wrenched open the cardboard flap in one ear-splitting rip, grabbed a bottle, twisted off the hissing top, and chugged the whole thing down in two seconds flat. He placed the bottle politely back in the box, pulled out another one, and chugged it, too. He nabbed a third and sat there gazing at the empty bottle for a moment. Then looked up at me, still standing in the doorway to my room, and grinned. "Well, old pal," he said, "the word is you've gotta drink about a case of this stuff to get anywhere." I laughed until my stomach hurt. Then I excused myself to the bathroom and vomited. I knew he would end up drinking again. He did, landing in his first rehab right before Ian's boarding school graduation, though he did manage to show up, looking wan and haunted, saying little.

Just after I graduated from college, Dad took me by surprise by asking me to visit him in New Mexico, where he'd bought a piece of property in Arroyo Seco, near Taos, with two casitas on it. He was still married to his second wife (the former secretary), but their union had been all but disemboweled: booze, brutality, bone-cracking hatred. This place was his refuge, where he could go to paint, to look at the mountains. Dad was in a great mood when I got there. To pay the mortgage, he said, he had rented out the lesser of the casitas to a "pack of do-gooders" hailing from Vermont. But there was a caveat: "I made it abundantly clear that if I sniff out any illicit drugs, I'm calling the cops and donating a grand to the Widows and Orphans

Fund to make sure that they take these little pricks on a one-way trip to the bottom of the Rio Grande." One day, however, he'd noticed that the license plate on the doomed renters' VW bus read BIKO, as in Stephen Biko, the slain South African civil rights activist. Not reading it correctly, he had perked up right away, and he strode over to the Vermonters, who were harvesting chili peppers in the front yard. My dad smiled widely, thumbing at the license plate. "Well, what do you know?" he chortled. "Booster Engine Cut Off!" I don't know if I have laughed so hard since. (After my dad died, the Peter Gabriel song "Biko," spookily, seemed to be playing everywhere. Or maybe I just heard it that way. "The outside world is black and white / with only one color: dead.")

After I had been at the casita for a few days, Dad paid me to go into town to eat by myself. He floated this gesture as a treat. It was an empty bluff. He wanted to drink the way he wanted to drink: alone. When I came back, he was passed out in a deck chair sitting behind an enormous telescope.

When I started my first job, in May 1991, I issued strict marching orders to myself: Work, work, work. Don't look up.

THREE

SAY YES:
LOVE AND MARRIAGE

I met Cal in the summer of 1991 at our first job after college, fact checkers for the now defunct *PC Magazine*. How I hated that job! I had a crushing chip on my shoulder: I couldn't believe that I had worked so hard to end up at a goddamned computer magazine with a bunch of loser computer people. I had done everything right! I had networked with and sent my résumé to editors at the major news, literary, and lifestyle magazines in New York (though with the first Bush recession in full swing, hiring freezes were entrenched). I had nurtured an ongoing correspondence with the then editor of *The New Yorker*, Bob Gottlieb, who showed me inexplicable kindness by responding to my fulsome notes on his manual typewriter and did his best to connect me with an entry-level editorial position, which was ultimately stymied by his ouster and the subsequent installation of the editorial impresario Tina Brown. In the end, the only job that offered to pay me a living wage, along with health insurance, was *PC Magazine* (the magazines for which I wanted to work—*Harper's, The New York Review of Books*—did not, which made working there a possibility only for smart kids bankrolled by their parents). So there I was, sullen and contemptuous, but also taking my career extremely seriously and studying office politics intently. I was like that self-absorbed, self-loathing, ineffectual, plotting guy in Dostoyevsky's *Notes from Underground*.

Cal, however, did not give a crap about any of that. He made this plain at our first introduction, in which he leaned back in his cubicle's office chair, drummed carelessly on his desk with a pencil, and allowed as how he had not only never networked with editors but didn't even really care, or know that much, about journalism. He had majored in religion and philosophy and was a hard-drinking member of the fraternity Beta Theta Pi. Having no clear idea of what he'd actually like to do for a career, he'd simply stuffed copies of his résumé into a few dozen envelopes addressed to "Human Resources" at various newspapers and magazines, gone on a handful of interviews, and taken the job at *PC Magazine* based on a vague sense that computers were "going to be important." He'd stay at the job, he said, until he got bored. "I told them that in my interview," he said. I was first dumbfounded, then seriously irritated. *Arrogant, not funny, not smart, frat guy,* I noted. *He'll be fired before summer is out.*

But, of course, I was wrong—as I daresay I have been about most important things in my life. In the first week of work, he appeared at the opening to my cubicle, panicked, to ask if I had any Windex. He needed it, he said, to disinfect a floppy disk that he suspected had a virus. I stared at him. I would come to recognize the look he had on his face then as his comic signature: a frozen deer-in-the-headlights expression, with an undercurrent of self-mockery. As I sat chomping on a giant liverwurst sandwich (which, he would later tell me, made him fall head over heels then and there), I mused: This guy is kinda pretty *funny.*

He also turned out to be an extremely quick study. Actually, he was flat-out *smart.* None of the fact checkers, including me, really knew anything about computers. As it turned out, most of us had been hired straight out of snooty liberal arts colleges because the management had decided that year to raise the editorial profile of *PC Magazine* by grooming fancy writers and editors rather than hiring techies for whom writing and editing was, essentially, irritating and trivial. Most of the twentysomethings in the fact-checking pool were English majors laboring to grasp even basic computerese, but within a few weeks of working there, Cal was using pliers to wrench chips off motherboards, tweaking macros, plugging in Ethernet networks. He had figured out exactly what was going on.

And he had a lot more going on besides that. I noted the dog-eared copy of Kierkegaard's *Either/Or* on his desk. I noted his good ties, unpleated khakis, chunky-knit sweaters. I noted that he was not just smart, but also a really good kind of weird. The turning point came when some computer company sent him a Rubik's Cube as PR swag along with a press kit, and I watched him solve it in under three minutes. When I expressed open admiration, he took off his shoes and socks and solved the thing with his prehensile toes. To me, it was like God speaking through the bush.

He also had a life, a fun life, which I did not. His social life was comprised of nightly bar gatherings of his fellow graduating class of fraternity brothers who had moved together en masse to the city that summer. He would come in to work bleary-eyed, but obviously content and well-adjusted: a normal recent college graduate. As an acid, chain-smoking malcontent with a past, I was obliged to deride him about that, which he accepted with good humor—and would later tell me that he had been "intrigued" by what he supposed was the secret, fascinating life that I was deliberately keeping private at work. (Again: It never fails to amaze how one's neuroses can, when masked, seem like something completely different to the outside world.) The truth was that I was isolated and miserable, living in a small apartment in a charmless netherworld wedged between the Upper East Side and Harlem with my extremely depressed room-mate. Most nights, I came home from work, holed up in my room, drank beer, and worked on short stories on my computer before passing out asleep on the petrified cotton strata embedded in my futon. It sucked. Did I mention Dostoyevsky?

Also, in spite of my perverse defensiveness, I admired Cal. Such confidence! Such was his breezy dignity and likeability that everyone instinctively conferred a virtually uncontested authority on him. I first observed it a few months after we met at work. As mentioned, when Cal and I were hired fresh out of college in 1991, *PC Magazine* was in the process of revamping its staff and structure from ragtag to professionally polished, and one of the executive moves was to hire a big gun from *Newsweek* to manage the crew of editorial assistants. The big gun, who was hired that winter, was going to train us to be real researcher-reporters. She immediately instituted a number of an-noying administrative changes, which involved attendance at daily progress meetings; files marked up and stapled together according to regulation; interminable accountability procedures that were impos-sible to follow and still get your actual work done. The changes stank, but the big gun herself also kind of stank. In retrospect, it's clear that she was put in a hostile situation that would have made anyone crabby. But her lording over us that this is how real reporters did it at *Newsweek* only reminded us that we were neither real re-porters nor employees of *Newsweek,* so the whole situation quickly became bad and contentious. Everyone groused about it during and after work and found passive-aggressive ways to undermine the whole operation—everyone, that is, except Cal.

He simply, coolly refused. The big gun would appear at his cubi-cle and ask him why he wasn't at the daily progress meeting. He would reply calmly, "I can't go to that meeting—I have too much work to do." Pretty soon, it became just so. Convinced by this argu-ment, the editor for whom he directly worked gave him special dispensation. Just like that, he became the only researcher-reporter who didn't have to attend the meetings. In fact, he didn't have to do anything except exactly what he wanted to do, and no one was exactly sure what that was, though he obviously was working. Cal had pulled off the ultimate Jedi mind trick. He was Obi-Wan Kenobi. He was Bartleby the Scrivener. He was the main guy in *Office Space*. He was my hero.

As evidenced at work, Cal's centrifugal force had a wide reach, but its nexus was at the center of his vast social circle. This is how it worked: He would begin taking calls every Friday, midmorning. The question was: "Where are we going tonight?" The answer was: wherever he wanted to go. This was not only because that was the place to go, but because that was where he would be. Every so often, there would be a defector who wanted to make some other suggestion, like a disgruntled populist. Cal would neither accede nor contest. He'd just say, "That's cool. Have a good time, man." Click. Occasionally, the defector might then decide to rally a coup, seizing the opportunity to lodge his resentment of Cal's benevolent despotism. There might be a sympathetic groundswell for a bit, but such was Cal's pull that it was just a matter of time before the kids came home to Daddy. The rebellion would fizzle out within a few hours, announced by the calls that would begin coming in a little after lunch: "Fuck Tenth Street Lounge, man. Where're we going?" I would not be surprised to learn that the East Village bar-club Brownies owed an impressive fraction of its popularity in the 1990s to Cal's influence.

But it wasn't his popularity that made such a big impression on me. For one thing, I like most people—I love a big handful of them—and by and large, the feelings have always seemed to be reciprocal. For another, being popular in your teens and early twenties is what it is for that period of time. I'm not sure that it says, in itself, a great deal about anything particularly durable in a person—and I am, as mentioned, someone for whom the secret of durable pigments means an inordinate amount. Rather, it was the quality of his friends' devotion that was so moving to me. This bespoke some important quality in him. I wasn't sure what that might be, but it seemed very good.

So in that mise-en-scène of early-twenties coolness, when he coolly began asking me to join him in hanging out with his friends after work, I coolly began considering it. In my timorous little heart, I was *psyched*. But of course I was also leery. First of all, there was the question of the friends. Historically, fraternity people and I are a bad fusion. The whole idea of a fraternity to me is dorky-ass at best, genuinely dangerous at worst. There was a better than excellent chance that I'd lose it at one or more of his friends, and that by morning I'd be crowned as "that uptight chick at your office." The other thing, of course, was that he was more than likely considering such invitations to be preliminary dates. Suffice it to say, there was no way I could do this. So I didn't go.

Cal was undeterred. He just said things like "You grabbing lunch? Hold on a sec—I'm starving." In fairly short order, he was accompanying me to Curry in a Hurry every day. He signed up for the corporate sponsored stop-smoking program that I had joined so that we could become stop-smoking "buddies." To help test our resolve, we were supposed to have meals together and rate the relative "tastiness" of after-eating cigarettes; soon, we were going out for dinner after work a few times a week. When that got pricey, he offered to make dinner for me at my apartment because I was a kitchen idiot. We went to art-house movies at the Film Forum and Angelika. After a while, I felt okay enough to get together with the fraternity friends, and they were not assholes. They were actually a whole crew of Harold and Kumar, and they would end up becoming close friends over the next sixteen years. I began saying things like "I'm not your girlfriend," and he would respond "What are you talking about?" Ultimately, we were hanging out together virtually every day and night. He would later confess that he hated Indian food and loved action-adventure blockbusters and that he had never had any intention of stopping smoking. But I had figured that out already. In truth, I had sniffed him out pretty much after the Windex incident. After that, I'd just been watching.

We finally got together at the office Christmas party. While our fellow fact checkers were either spazzing at the office party shuffle or throwing up behind the open bar, we drank way too many pints of Bass and sat at a table with a yellow rose on it. He gave it to me; I rolled my eyes. We left the party in a cab and never left each other's side for the next sixteen years. I kept the yellow rose for ten years, until it crumbled to dust.

What did we do in the early love period? We mooned over each other in cafés in the West Village. Say all you want about that backdrop—I didn't care then, and I don't care now. We clearly observed the clichéd stage set of our budding romance. We giggled about it. Look—here we are, huddled together under the awning of a French pastry shop on Bleeker as rain gushes onto the cobblestone street! Look—red carnations in the vase atop the red-and-white-checked tablecloth at our Italian restaurant! Look—we can't read the Sunday *Times* and our lattes have gotten tepid because we're too absorbed in the semiotics of each other's every facial expression! So what? It was lovely and beautiful, and I have never felt more swaddled in happiness and ease. I even remember reading *Bonfire of the Vanities* at the time: Sherman McCoy recalling the early days with the woman who would become his wife, living in the squalor of their West Village studio, happy and hopeful in spite of their relative poverty. And I remember thinking: *Yuppie scum—only a matter of time before that guy becomes a bond trader.* To be young and in love in New York is clichéd if you have illusions about yourself, the world: that things will change. We had no illusions. No one was going to be rich. We didn't like our jobs. He was a good person masquerading as a frat guy–partier; I knew it. I was a genuine freak masquerading as a poser; he knew it. That was immutable. We were giddy and hopeful anyway.

We were giddy and hopeful in spite of the odd truth that we didn't have much in common. Although I mostly got over it, after I came to really like the actual guys themselves, his fraternity affiliation remained a bee in my bonnet, albeit a bee that buzzed more lethargically over time. His love of Anne Rice, even of Kierkegaard, came close to being deal-breakers in the very early stages. *Interview with the Vampire* and *Diary of a Seducer* struck me as frothy, grandiose, reductive—teenage Goth. There were other things. I do not like most action-adventure movies. I do like adventures on the spur of the moment. I do not think Winona Ryder is a good actor, though I do think she is beautiful. I do think Chris Farley was one of the funniest people who ever lived, though I do not think that it had anything to do with his weight. I love John Updike, Vladimir Nabokov, William Faulkner, Raymond Carver, and Douglas Coupland. I hate cats, bands whose lead female singers have girlish voices, black furniture, and blue jokes. I am afraid of bills, parking tickets, and pretty much anything involving mail and money. I am not afraid of speaking up or of working super, extra hard to get a job that I love. I am an unconscionable slob. He was the exact opposite in every regard, except with the blue humor. But none of that really mattered. Discovering his lack of interest in, or downright aversion to, the things I liked actually made me feel valued and safe. He had done these things to be near me, with me: not the résumé me, the snarky, fashiony me, the wounded animal me. *Me.* I felt happy, calm, protected. I would be freaking out about whatever issue of the day, and he would sit back, regard me as a painting, and have something marvelous and soothing and right to say that made everything make sense.

I wasn't the only one to whom he extended such consolation, though I may have been the most reliant on it and, because of that, the most grateful. His friends ran everything by him before making a move on virtually anything. They wanted to know: Should they go to graduate school? What kind of soap should they use—Lever 2000 or Dial? Where should they take someone on the second date—McSwiggen's or ice skating at Rock Center? Where should they live—cheap Kip's Bay, cheap East Village? Hair: gel or mousse? They even asked him for medical advice, though he cannot abide blood, sweat, or innards. They asked him for investment advice, though he has never picked a good stock. No woman ever became the official girlfriend of a friend without meeting Cal first. That his friends adored him certainly explains a great deal of this, but it was more than that, as I had surmised early on. People *trusted* Cal. His principles were so ingrained that he never thought to advertise them. They were just knitted into the bones.

I had never known anyone like this; such traits seemed practically unaccountable. But the great cosmic ledger keeps track of every credit and debit, and the receipt for Cal's solid soul and infallible ethics were from the same place: his upbringing.

Cal loved his parents. Period. Early in our togetherness, I thought this was some kind of goody-goody bluff. On my home world, you had to say that you loved your parents, but you remained ambivalent, guarded, and critical. I learned quickly that Cal was a different animal. One time, I pouted dramatically about his having made a plan to have dinner with his parents one evening rather than eat with me, though he ate with me every night. He looked at me square-on and said that his parents had done everything for him, he loved them, and that if they wanted to have dinner with him every week, he would be happy to do it. I was so moved that though I didn't understand it, I never said anything about it again. But over the years, I was able to assemble the papyrus pieces of Cal's Genesis story. It was like decoding extraterrestrial hieroglyphics.

Cal came from family people. They were from the Philippines, and to the extent that it is fair or plausible to generalize, one can say of Filipino society that it is extraordinarily devoted to family—and for this reason, getting to know Cal's was disorienting and provoking for a rogue entity like me. At first, I thought it was a question of size. While his nuclear family comprised just Cal, his younger sister, and his parents, such restrictive definitions were not observed in their worldview; anyone related to them was family. This is a tradition in a huge number of cultures, but even so, Cal's family was downright galactic: twenty aunts and uncles, more than ninety first cousins, an extended circle of grands, great-grands, second and third cousins, their spouses, and so on. Except for a handful who'd stayed in the Philippines, they all lived on Staten Island, and they spent all their free time together. Family dinners, for example, were like nothing I'd ever seen.

In my WASP experience, if you were invited to a family dinner, you expected to be offered a cocktail or two and submit to the parents' tactful interview about your background, education, occupation, and interests, after which you would sit down to a pleasant conversation and the stock Protestant "guest" meal: poached salmon, asparagus, and if someone was feeling fancy, maybe risotto with a barely discernible amount of butter and salt. With Cal's family, there might be four people present, there might be fifty. As soon as you walked in the door, you were kissed on the cheek with an audible smack, exhorted to "Eat first!" and tendered a Styrofoam plate groaning with *pancit palabok, lumpia, lechon, tapa,* and rice. After that, you were on your own. You sat wherever there was an open spot, eating, smiling, watching the children dash about and make impromptu performances for the adults, who laughed and clapped their hands and absently admonished the little girls to straighten their dresses and the little boys to "be nice!" After the card tables were set up, the mah-jongg sets and whiskey bottles came out, and as the night wore on, more relations would simply show up. At some point, an auntie would plunk herself down at the white baby grand and produce the most perfect, tinkling cocktail piano you've ever heard outside of an old-school hotel bar, and before long, a tipsy coterie would encircle her singing "You Light Up My Life," "Memories," and "Love Will Keep Us Together," swaying in unison, eyes glossy with sentiment.

I had no idea how to operate in such entropic circumstances. What was I supposed to do? No parental figure engaged me in one-on-one chitchat; no one wanted the abstract of my curriculum vitae; no one was interested in my opinion of lobbyists or right-wing media. Didn't Cal's family want to get to know me? If nothing else, my ability to sustain polite conversation was, I felt, one of my assets. If they didn't ask me questions, how would I be able to charm them—to win them over? "That's just not how they are," shrugged Cal. "Don't take it personally." But I did take it personally.

Cal's mother and I struggled in particular. I thought she was sexist, ostentatious, and anti-intellectual, and I'm pretty sure that she thought I was a slut, a dangerous liberal (a "women's libber," she spat), and a smart-ass. But after about five years or so of Cal's and my being together, a turning point materialized at one of these giant, jolly family get-togethers. As I squished in at the edge of the crowded piano stool munching *lumpia* and warbling "Love Me Tender" in between bites, I realized that I loved pretty much everyone there. I had taken a particular shine to Cal's youngest cousin, a troubled, sickly little boy who was so bright and ridiculously sweet that I couldn't help eating him up. Two of Cal's other cousins, a seriously smart and exceptionally kind pair of high school sisters, were dazzling: It never occurred to me that teenagers could be so uncloyingly cooperative and well-adjusted. To me, these girls were flat-out perfect, the kind of kids everyone hopes to have; I invented internships for them at the magazine for which I worked so that they could beef up their résumés for college admissions, and they were nothing but a pleasure. I loved all these children's mothers. And, it struck me, I loved Cal's mother.

First, we had discovered a passion in common: clothes and bargain shopping. That broke the ice. But once we discovered our mutual respect for hard work and self-determination, our suspicion of each other began to melt away. I learned that as new émigrés to the United States, Cal's mother had worked the night shift as a nurse to support the family while his father studied for the foreign medical exams. Exhausted but practical, she had trained Cal, from age six, to vacuum, sort laundry, and cook for the family. Everyone had done what needed to be done—that's what family does, *di ba*? When she learned that I'd had to sue my wealthy father to go to college, she hooted in disbelief: Who ever heard of such a thing? His own flesh and *blood*! And I still talked to him? *Ano*, it was that *woman*, that *wife*—she was greedy, she had poisoned his mind. Your father does not appreciate what a good daughter he has! But don't worry, dar-*ling*, what comes around goes around—believe *me*. You work hard, and God will provide for you. My eyes would well up in astonishment at her heart for me. How could I *not* love her?

There was something else that I realized, too. Cal's family never really cared much about my, or anyone's, pedigree, level of achievement, or personal appeal, unless such things had a practical application, such as drawing a higher salary than one would have been able to command otherwise. What mattered to them was: Do you love this family? Are you willing to help its members? If you proved that your answer was "Yes," that's all they cared about. You could be a gas station attendant or a drug addict, and though they'd push you to better yourself if you were, there was no question that you'd have the unqualified support of this enormous, tight network at your back. If you failed to appear at a gathering, family would phone you relentlessly or come in person to fetch you. If you became ill, family would be at your bedside, feeding you, keeping you company. If you needed money, family would loan you what they had, put in calls to find you a job. No one ever used a babysitter. You would never, ever be alone. It took the wind right out of me when this dawned on me. Imagine: never alone.

But in truth, the family togetherness trait had never truly meshed with Cal's own temperament. Even as a little boy, while the whole tribe was in peak festive mode, Cal would duck into his room or, if they were at a relative's home, under a table, and burrow into a book. His mother would rattle his cage in frustration and insist that he join the party, but Cal didn't want to; he preferred his own cerebral solitude. "He was always rea*ding,* rea*ding,* rea*ding!*" his mother would tell me, as if this were a sign of some shocking character defect. "He never wanted to be with his family—my son is a lo*ner!*" There was not a single other person like this, not in the hundreds of family members. Cal also did not dance, another anathema in his family and, one could fairly assert, in Filipino culture at large. Let me tell you something: You may think that you have danced and that you're maybe pretty good at it, but that is probably because you have never been to a real Filipino wedding. *Everybody* dances, and everybody rocks it like you would not *believe*—from eighteen months to ninety-six years, it doesn't matter. Not Cal. So even though he was accepted, Cal was also regarded as something of a mutant. In addition, however, as the firstborn of his generation and the first to have truly grown up as an American, he was regarded as a special authority, an envoy. So even as he was browbeaten by his mother into family togetherness, and ordered in no uncertain terms to be a doctor when he grew up, he was also invariably consulted in all official family matters involving transactions with the outside world. Cal rather liked this position, especially since it gave him the appearance of being involved and, moreover, deflected attention from his retreats to be alone.

Even with his hermetic inclinations, however, Cal clearly radiated the confidence that comes only with a sense of belonging; it was central to his ease in the world. But so was his parents' marriage. Unlike mine and most of our friends', Cal's parents not only were still together but were a unified, happy couple. The secret to this, I think, is that they didn't see themselves as being in a relationship; they saw themselves as husband and wife. This still strikes me as a revolutionary notion, having been raised, like most people my age, alongside the Boomerish zeitgeist that marital cohesion is reliant on individual fulfillment. It is tempting to chalk this up to a Filipino family ethos, but that would be cheap and false: There was always a lot of conjugal drama gusting about the family, including children born out of wedlock and rampant cheating. But not Cal's parents. They genuinely loved each other and were always together; they genuinely loved Cal, and Cal loved them. Although he had rebelled against the family business by not becoming a doctor, and against the family culture by not becoming a confirmed Catholic, Cal had never been one of those teenagers who, like me and my type, shunned their parents at puberty's onset, leaning on their friends, boyfriends, or girlfriends to fill the gaps. He hadn't needed to.

Perhaps that's why, to this day, no one has ever heard him make anything resembling a degrading remark about a woman or about women in general. Maybe this doesn't sound like a big deal, and it never seemed like such a big deal to me in all the years that we were together. But I have since learned how surprisingly disgusting a great many men are when they think that women aren't listening—or even sometimes in their presence. Cal was never this way. It just wasn't in him.

There is a story that underscores that point, a story that endeared him to me in a way he never could have guessed when he related it years ago. After graduating from college, Cal had gone on one of those epic backpacking trips across Europe, the kind in which you stay in hostels, ride the EuroRail, and meet all kinds of other people in their early twenties from different countries who are doing the same thing. One of the main purposes of these trips, aside from becoming a cultured person who has visited Europe, is to hook up.

So there he was in Florence. He toured the Duomo, the Uffizi, and the Medici chapels, and he met an attractive, interesting, smart young woman whose next stop was Athens. But Cal's plan was to go to Venice. "Come with me to Athens!" urged the young woman. "We'll take the train together—it'll be fun!" It sounded like fun. It probably would have been fun. But his plan was to go to Venice. "So, change your plans—come on!" she prodded. Knowing him as I do, I can visualize this scene perfectly. He is standing there, itinerary clutched tightly, staring at her, vibrating with inner conflict. He knows exactly what this invitation means, knows that he will be an errant idiot not to take her up on it, that his friends will ridicule him into a sliver of a man, that he will come to regret it in middle age. But he has made a plan to go to Venice. And that plan is fixed as deeply in his psyche as the Duomo is in the piazza. "I'm sorry," he said, "but I planned to go to Venice." When he told me this story, I knew that I would never meet a better man than this.

But in terms of our particular relations, this story came to illustrate two things as time went on. First, sex would never be a major point of connection. Even in the beginning, when people are supposed to be having sex in all manner of unhygienic places, we were more into cuddling, talking, and hanging out than getting it on. Was it a warning sign? At the time, I told myself it was the hallmark of a secure, mature relationship. For one thing, I had already had my share of having sex in bathrooms, stairwells, cars, and barns with Jai. People in adult relationships, I told myself, did not have that kind of sex. Their lives were not about the kind of world in which sex like that thrives. People in stable, mature relationships had careers to construct, process, and endure. They had ideas that they felt were important enough to make real. They had an interesting, vital circle of friends with whom they went out drinking and to late dinners. They had eclectic, even pedantic, music collections; favorite contemporary writers; good parties in walk-up apartments. This was the stuff of real relationships. Id-crazy, soul-gluing sex didn't seem to be a part of this mix.

That's what I told myself at the time. What was closer to the truth was that sex had become in my mind synonymous with giving myself away completely. It was my ultimate trading card: You can have me, if you can protect and envelop me. And by the time I met Cal, I never wanted to sacrifice myself again: I wanted to work, to make something more of myself than a patched-up rag doll. I had the feeling, from the outset, that this would be a possibility with him, that he would not make soul-sapping demands of me, that I would not have to sacrifice myself to be a real, self-determining entity. I was right. I did not see then that this is what he had always wanted, too, nor did I understand the loneliness inherent in such a bargain.

The second, and ultimately the most important, point of the Venice story was this: It simply never occurred to Cal to allow his moral compass to be pulled in any direction other than his own. Me, I would have given anything to *have* a moral compass, my sentient planet's missing piece of equipment. My center, to the extent that I had one, had never held. It was more like a hazmat container for high-pressure gas. Reading *Heart of Darkness* in my junior year of high school, I'd felt an instant, horrible sense of kinship with Kurtz. The wilderness had found me out early, too—and it echoed loudly within because I, too, was hollow at the core. The major difference between Kurtz and me was that I was too afraid to allow the horrifying nihilism that lived inside me to penetrate the membrane of my persona, which talked all the time and liked clothes. A line from a Billy Bragg song sums it up: "a little black cloud in a dress." Though I was nothing but dark wind, I was desperate to feel something of solidity, to feel that there was somehow real ore embedded in my heart's gusty caves. I wanted that moral compass. I didn't have the first idea of how to get one. In hindsight, I simply allowed myself to be drawn to his. He did not seem to mind. Without him, I was gas; without me, he was rock. Together, we were a world.

There were fissures from the start. But they were the kind that might have mended themselves had the pieces been broken in the right places to begin with. If you buy Plato's take on soulmates—that they are two halves of a whole, split before birth and searching for their mate to fit back together—then you might reason that, perhaps in our case, the severing of our particular pieces was never in our own control. The Greeks, it seems, get you coming or going.

At the end of our first year together, I had moved away from him, from New York to Washington, D.C. It was 1992, and I said that I wanted to see if I couldn't capitalize on some of that Clintonian "youthquake" energy and muscle my way into writing for *The Washington Post.* I honestly hated my job at *PC Magazine,* and though I tried to piggyback on Cal's workplace detachment—as well as his (correct) long view that by working at the magazine of record for the industry that was going to dominate for the next decade, we would cement our stature in it—I could not drum up an enthusiastic rhythm in my everyday process. This wasn't a problem for Cal: He was okay with going to work, doing the work, then either going out with friends or going home, kicking back, and watching TV. I envied him this. I wanted to be able to kick back, *needed* to kick back, and Cal's congenital ability to do it was one of the reasons that I was drawn to him.

But I couldn't do it. For one thing, I hated how much TV he watched. I hated that it was virtually impossible to get away from it in that small apartment. It's not that I'm one of those people who think that television is the devil. Actually, that's a lie: I do think it is the devil. With a few programming exceptions, I have always been deeply unsettled by this eerie sensation I have in front of the TV—that my life force is being siphoned off and replaced with a pornified marinade of human drama, history, current events, the natural world. Furthermore, I'm a spaz. While I am a standard-issue Generation X person in many ways (and like all Generation X people, I am ashamed of that), I have never been big on inertia. While we all know by now that, yes, X was never *actually* apathetic but just inconsolably disappointed, most of us at least had the appearance, the gestalt, of slackerishness. I'm way too antsy for that. If I don't like something, it's very hard for me to sit still and be quiet. I have to do something about it. Right now. So, one weekday evening as we lay on his couch watching something on TV, I had the premonition that I would lie on this couch, night after night, looking away every so often and becoming instantly dreadstruck by the void of my life, and then being pulled back into that numbing, low-level seizure induced by whatever happened to be blipping on the screen, and the exact words flashed into my mind: *When I am dead, I won't have to make decisions.* That was it. I bolted to D.C. within the month.

But I did not see this as a breakup. Cal, though hurt by my rash decision, did not, either. We would simply stay together at a distance. At the time, I didn't know what it was that kept a couple together, but it is fair to say that some degree of thermodynamics is necessary to inspire, and certainly to sustain, mutual pull. Cal and I didn't have it. In hindsight, I might have been instinctively trying to generate some by putting space between us. Certainly, our physical separation did nothing to unravel our attachment. During the two years that I lived in Washington, we talked on the phone at least three times a day and spent at least two weekends each month together. I never even considered cheating. Neither did he. But the absence of heat persisted.

It's not as though it never came up. On the rare occasions that we discussed it, we did so gingerly. I would not push, because I could not lose him. He was afraid to push because he did not want to rip apart any delicate stitching that our relationship had lent to my open, raw psyche. He had not known that it was possible to come from the kind of world from which I came; learning of it made him protective, but it also scared him. On my twenty-second birthday, Cal had gifted me with *Laughable Loves* by Milan Kundera. He told me that I reminded him of the main female character in *The Unbearable Lightness of Being.* "Who?" I wanted to know, already knowing that it would be Sabina, Tomas's mistress, the boho artist, the one with the hat. Actually, no, he said. I reminded him of Tereza. Oh. The heavy-hearted innocent, the "child put in a basket and sent downstream" for Tomas to find—the one who hated anything to do with bodies, who cleaved to absolutism, who was crushed by the demolition of her values. The only one Tomas truly loved in spite of her asexuality, the one who ballasted his lightness with her heaviness. I nodded. He wasn't far off. But he was also miles away.

I wouldn't have known how to say this at the time, but I now know that it is possible for someone to be damaged without being breakable. Heat can cauterize: It can keep two people soldered to-gether when forces on all sides are pulling them apart. Sex *is* soul-gluing in a loving relationship, it *is* essential. It is what separates friends from mates. It populates empty planets.

But I didn't really get that at the time. I just knew something was wrong, and I would flailingly try to fix it every so often during the two years we were living apart. Sometimes during our bimonthly vis-its I would, in drunken states, hurl myself at him, and while the veloc-ity of it would simulate ardor, it was never long before it was exposed as a simile, leaving both of us sad, confused, and embarrassed. My re-sponse was to whip myself up into a state of constant kinetic energy. I wrote for *The Washington Post,* for Time-Life Books, for *Glamour,* for every publication that would have me. I jammed every potentially vacant moment with work or social connection that was related to lining up more work. I made hundreds of genial, interesting acquain-tances during that period in D.C. but no durable friendships. I lived in a house with five other people, but I essentially lived by myself. I slept in winks. I might have heaved myself into his outermost orbit by moving to D.C., but Cal was still my center of gravity. I had to move back to New York, I came to realize, or I would be forever lost.

When I returned, we moved in together, but my manic kinesis in-tensified. Cal's career, in my view, was stagnating. He was still work-ing at the same place, still vaguely interested in it but admittedly not passionate about it. He still did not seem to care much about his ca-reer, and while his relative inertia was alien to me as ever, I had come, in a way, to rely on it because I did care. I cared about work in the way the lone figure adrift on the life raft cares about not being eaten by sharks or dying of dehydration. Throughout my twenties, I lived in a sustained state of panic, some of it ostensibly work-related, all of it insidiously self-absorbed. Like the hapless protagonist in some form of *Sex and the City*–style Greek tragedy, I had left New York because I hated writing about technology only to return to write about it again, but this time for a major newsweekly. So I just went on torture rampages.

Was I going to make my deadline? Had I interviewed everyone I could have interviewed? Did I get that iffy part of the fifth paragraph right? Did I file the right caption with the right picture or the left picture? I hate myself. I hate every little thing: how self-absorbed, how empty and small I am. My mother was right: I'm a "miserable failure," an "evil child." Guess what? I was promoted! The youngest senior editor at *U.S. News & World Report*! Check me the fuck *out*! Now I'm all over TV! Uh-oh, now there's a new editor boss, and he hates me. Is he out to get me, or just impervious and grumpy? Why does he hate me? Do you think I'll ever be promoted again? I am an incompetent, a fraud, a pathetic fucking joke. Everyone can see it. The boss can see it. I don't know why you're with me; I don't know why anyone would be with me. My father is gone. *Gone*. But I can be funny! Can't I be kind of funny? I can be funny, right? Why was I writing about technology? I hated technology! I want to be writing for the theater! Now I'm writing about technology *and* I'm writing a play. My play isn't finished yet. My play sucks. But now I've been offered my own TV show! My editor is mad at me because I'm writing a play and have my own TV show, even though I'm still getting my work done for the magazine. I am terrified because everyone hates me, and you are going to leave me because I'm such a lunatic. Why wouldn't you? Why wouldn't anybody? My father left me. Left me. Was my editor going to fire me because, even though he didn't say it, he obviously felt that there was no way I could write a play, have my own TV show, and get my work done? I can't believe I just spent three hundred dollars on a pair of shoes. I spend money on clothes because I hate myself. But don't they look kind of good?

Much of this is the boilerplate raving of any neurotic writer living in New York. It was accompanied by a consuming sense of incompetence, fraudulence, plain badness. I was sure that I wasn't the person I'd advertised myself to be. Deadliest: I was my father. I panicked, suffered, and often drank late into the night with Cal talking me down. And he did, he always talked me down. Because perhaps the most extraordinary thing about Cal was his ability to step back, out, above, and zero in on what was extraordinary about virtually any-thing. He zeroed in on facets of me that I did not perceive, that per-haps were not even there but for his perception of them. I was, he said, the most amazing person he had ever known. I cared, he said, I wanted to do better, and no matter what had happened to me, I never gave up, I kept moving. Look, he said, at what you have made, what you have always made, out of *nothing*. Magic, he told me. *You are magic, Susie.*

In college, I had taken an astrophysics class, harboring the small, ultimately fatuous ambition that the night sky might open itself up to me again, and while the results were catastrophic, I did grasp a few things. One of them was that there is a force called inertial force, also known as fictitious force or pseudo force. It appears to be a force, and it can even be treated mathematically like one. But it is not a real force. It is produced by the reaction of a body to an accelerating force, lasting only as long as the accelerating force does.

I kept moving.

For the first several years that Cal and I were together, my father was so poisonously alcoholic that he was not really a person. In that period, he went through three harrowing rehabs. I had attended each one, crippled after each of his failures. Cal could not understand why I wanted anything to do with him; *he* certainly didn't. You sit there freaking out every day, expecting to get a call that he's either blown his head off or killed someone? When you work up the nerve to call him, the guy can hardly ever be bothered to talk to you—and when he does, you're crying for a week afterward because he's pounded you into the pavement?

I had a recurring dream in which my dad had killed The Edge of U2; I had to find Bono and beg his forgiveness. I would tell Cal about these dreams, weeping. *Jesus,* he would say, shaking his head. *But you'd really like him if you met him sober,* I would say; *he really is great.* What can you say? Alcoholism.

There was a period after the third rehab during which my dad did stay sober. I told myself not to hope for too much, but of course I did. It didn't last. But in that period of about two years when he was in between wives, Dad was back. He had moved into a fishing cottage on the coast of Massachusetts that sat perched atop a cliff abutting the ocean. It was perfect for my dad: all that roil outside, the coziness inside, the solitude. And he *was* great. He was himself: contemplative, sparky, full of ideas, so funny it made you cry. The first time he invited us up to visit him in his cottage, my prediction materialized: Cal and Dad were instant comrades.

They were both into cryptozoology, UFOs, and conspiracy theories, and they stirred each other into a froth, trading reports and specious factoids about all kinds of crackpot bullshit. My job was to appear disdainfully amused, chime in from time to time about how ludicrous such interests were, be swatted down, and ultimately be praised for indulging their foolishness (and pitied for being a nonbeliever). Then the conversation turned to football. It was definitely a classic piece of sexist theater, but I didn't mind. I was just so happy that Dad was Dad again and that Cal could finally see what I'd been talking about.

But perhaps the most revelatory moment during the visit was Dad's introducing us to the "Carlin Room." When we arrived, Dad gave us a tour of his place, which, though small compared to the house we'd lived in outside Philadelphia or the McMansion he and his second wife had remodeled in the Boston suburbs, still could easily have accommodated a family of five. Dad wanted nothing to do with that. The master bedroom was taken, of course; the bedroom with the best light he made his painting studio; the one downstairs was his home office. But the remaining one, the largest one, he called the Carlin Room. The thing was actually padlocked, and, Dad forewarned us—with one raised, bushy red eyebrow—dead-bolted on the inside.

The Carlin Room was so named for an old bit from the young George Carlin in which he proclaimed that the chief function of one's room is to protect your "stuff," that one's "stuff"—and keeping everyone's grubby hands off it—ranked chief among the most primal of human needs. Carlin went on further to expound on the paradox of "shit" and "stuff," explaining (and I paraphrase): "Have you ever noticed that whenever you go to other people's houses their stuff is shit, and your shit is stuff?" The Carlin Room, my dad explained, was the only room in the entire house that was exclusively his. No one was allowed in it; no one was allowed to *look* into it; no one was even allowed to *think* about looking in it. It was, he grouched, "where I keep my *stuff*, man."

It would have been folly to point out to my dad that he lived alone and rarely had visitors, and even if he had, there was no guest room where they might stay because he had claimed the entire house as exclusively his already. Not that I didn't point this out anyway. If there was ever a man who required a good-hearted roasting to a crisp on a spit, it was Dugal Thomas. I saw it as my duty to stand and deliver it, mostly because, so far as I know, no one else would. But while he mostly enjoyed my skewerings, if he was in the right frame of mind, I was only able to sear the surface; his insides always remained raw. If the Carlin Room could talk, which it did via my dad's every gesture, it would have bawled the state motto of New Hampshire: Live Free or Die! I didn't bat an eye when he actually did move to New Hampshire two years later, holed up by a lake with an arsenal of shotguns and handguns and his third wife. (My brother and I cracked up when, in the mid-nineties—when Dad was still living alone in Massachusetts—the FBI started closing in on the identity and whereabouts of the Unabomber. *Thank God Dad is dyslexic,* we said, *because that Unabomber guy is doing it on a manual typewriter, and he's a good speller. If spell-check was involved in any one of those communiqués, Dad'd be in a lockdown at Quantico.*)

As Cal and I were driving home from the trip, I was hyperfocused on the great time I'd had and greedily probed Cal for a report on what a great time he'd had. Cal was quiet. Then he said, "Dugal is a great guy—I can see why you thought I'd like him." The "but" dangled from its precipice. I pushed it. "That 'Carlin Room' says a lot," he said. "There's a fundamental selfishness about your dad. He'll always be alone because of it."

That Dad was an alcoholic, a charming bastard, a self-absorbed prick, a dilettante, the tragic hero in the story of his own life (and mine) were all facts that had been as firmly established as my social security number or the city of my birth. But they were the kinds of character assignments one makes to establish a cast list to which you can refer when you forget why certain people are acting in certain ways. They are useful name tags, but they don't do much to describe emotional reality. Cal had done it. He had absorbed my father's essence: alone.

That was not going to be me.

What can anyone say that the Greeks haven't said in three dozen ways already? Did I end up strong-arming Cal into becoming a sexless caregiver? I foam with remorse and self-loathing at the thought.

I did not enter marriage with such intentions. In one way, my expectations were coincident with everyone else's. According to research, Generation X does, by an overwhelming majority—94 percent—look first for a "soulmate" in marriage, and 86 percent expect to find theirs.* I had found mine. Like my peers from divorced households, I entered marriage with the presumption that Cal and I were going to outdo my parents altogether. After all, we'd already been together for nearly eight years before getting married—even though divorce rates are up to 48 percent higher for those who have lived together first than for those who haven't.† There was no question in my mind that we would beat those odds. Part of the reason this happens, I think, is that many people our age consider it old-

* Pamela Paul, *The Starter Marriage and the Future of Matrimony* (New York: Villard Books, 2002).
† Ibid.

fashioned and naïve to think that marriage fundamentally changes a person, especially if you lived with your spouse out of wedlock beforehand; the essential dynamic is entrenched, and there seems little reason to expect innovation. Moreover, while everyone acknowledges that even though the big bridey moment is exhilarating, fabulous, swelling with feeling, it also represents something of a media marketing benchmark and therefore has the patina of a sham. The X subtext on the wedding day celebration is, be clear-eyed; enjoy the moment, but remember that it's only a day; after that, you go back to the relationship.

The Relationship. By all accounts, no American generation has been more devoted to attending to the every nuance of The Relationship than X. We are, say sociologists, anthropologists, and other manner of cultural observers, more emotionally invested in our spouses than previous generations were in theirs; our marriages are deep friendships and genuine partnerships. We depend on each other and work together. Because of all these things, adultery, for example, is far more devastating for us than it was for our parents or grandparents. Indeed, it's fascinating to look at studies of this, because the generational attitudes toward sex and commitment are so profoundly different that some researchers muse that they may suggest that an evolutionary change is taking place in male and female *brains* under our very noses. In a 2003 study, the late Baltimore psychologist Shirley Glass, Ph.D., a specialist in infidelity research (and also the mom of the awesome Ira Glass, host of public radio's *This American Life*), found that the mores of sexual infidelity were metamorphosing, in epic proportions. The traditional standard for men—love is love and sex is sex—is essentially dying out. Increasingly, men and women are developing serious emotional attachments long before they commit adultery.

"The sex differences in infidelity are disappearing," reported Glass in a 2003 *Psychology Today* interview. "In my original 1980 study, there was a high proportion of men who had intercourse with almost no emotional involvement at all—nonrelational sex. Today, more men are getting emotionally involved." Historically, the strictly sexual tryst didn't have any effect on men's marital satisfaction. "You could be in a good marriage and still cheat," explained Glass. But the new adultery, she found, was not just disruptive but more likely catastrophic, ending in divorce. The betrayal is simply so profound that it destroys everything. Moreover, what was fascinating from an anthropological point of view was that this new pattern constituted a major hit to a long-standing male code. "The double standard for adultery is disappearing," declared Rutgers University anthropologist Helen Fisher, Ph.D., in the same *Psychology Today* article. "It's been around for 5,000 years and it's changing in our lifetime. It's quite striking. Men used to feel that they had the right. They don't feel that anymore."

One can only wonder if this change has been brought about by X's fundamentally different view of romantic relationships. That is, it seems clear that we don't have the old-school sense of "Oh, well— men will be men" or "Coo-coo-ka-choo, Mrs. Robinson," but rather: *You're my best friend, my It—how could you even have thought about doing this to me?* So, is it any surprise that 94 percent of Generation Xers expect to marry our soulmates? Given that, how could we stand to think that our relationships with our partners are temporal, potentially dissoluble? I couldn't—any more than I can grasp the mortality of our own solar system.

But after observing Cal's parents, I wanted something else. I wanted what they had. I wanted to be transformed. Within a few months of our getting married, I stopped drinking. Drinking had made me a self-revolving twister, and I realized that if I continued I would never be able to approach having a real marriage but would persist in ripping everything up and heaving it around the countryside. People say that you should make such epic changes for yourself, not for others, but I was, frankly, tired of myself. I wanted Cal to have *his* turn having problems, if he wanted to have some, and I wanted to be there to help him with them. I wanted him to have *his* turn at a career to which he could devote himself. He had already gotten seed money to launch an online investment advising company and was working passionately, for the first time in his life, to get it off the ground. I was excited for him, I was proud of him. I wanted him to know that I was actually there, as his wife, not as a messy, rebellious child. I wanted to be a *wife*.

FOUR

ALIVE AND KICKING:
HAVING CHILDREN

For our wedding, my stepsister had given Cal and me a curious gift: a joint astrological chart. She was a student of a big-deal astrologer in Boulder and had contracted with him to record on audio-cassette his interpretations of our celestial intersection. It was easily the most awesome wedding present we got. Cal and I had elected to listen to these interpretations via the tape player of my father-in-law's midlife-crisis red Porsche, screaming down I-95 to a friend's wedding in Virginia. On the tape, the guy told us that our chart said that I liked to talk a lot (really?) and that after a long period of stagnation, Cal's career was revving up. But what our joint stars had highlighted in yellow marker, he said, was not only that we were going to have children, but that we would feel that being parents together fulfilled our potential as human beings. Moreover, being parents together was *the* big cosmic purpose of our relationship.

The big cosmic purpose! This was great news, to me, anyway. There had never been any question in my mind that in spite of everything, I would have children. Certainly very little about my background and behavior indicated that I would be well suited to raising them; indeed, nothing did. I can't say that I ever had fantasies about being The Mom, but for as long as I could remember, I had always feelings of rightness—of happy inevitability—whenever I thought about having children of my own. Had I been called on to articulate these impulses at the time, however, my answer would have been that I knew that Cal would be a perfect father—and that together, we would be able to right the karmic injustices of my own childhood. We would make other mistakes, for sure. But we would not do what my parents did.

Cal, however, wasn't so sure—not about whether we would do a good job, but whether he wanted to have kids at all. His chief concern, sweetly, was that he and I would drift apart, that our connection would erode consequent to the calcifying effects of daily domestic life. We didn't know it then, but it was just before I got pregnant that Cal and I had a moment that I can still feel embedded in my gut like a little shard of shrapnel. We were on a walk in Prospect Park near our Park Slope, Brooklyn, apartment, and after a while of contented, silent strolling, Cal stopped. "This is what I mean," he said, looking at me. "I don't want everything to be so different that we lose *this*." I took his hand. "It will be *better*," I said. "It will be *more* than this."

Not long after listening to the astrological wedding tape, I was pregnant. And the planning began. Like most people who have never had children, I had pretty firm ideas about how to raise them. The plan was that I would take the standard American maternity leave of six weeks, Cal and I would find a good nanny or day-care center, and I would then resume my regular twelve-hour workday as a journalist. Why wouldn't I? Why wouldn't anyone? My temperament is such that I emerged from the womb a feminist, hardly a rebellious genetic mutation in my clan. While all the women in my family would wish to be, and would be, described as "ladies"—with their unimpeachable style and manners—my mother always worked, as did her mother, and their mothers and aunties, all academics. I had always felt proud of them for it, felt that I had been given excellent examples of how work could not just support a woman but enrich her, too. Plus, not only did I like my work, I was also not sure that hanging out with a baby all day long would be my thing. Kids, yes; babies, don't know. My mother had warned me that babies were mind-numbingly boring for anyone with a handful of brains; she urged me to line up a baby nurse at once. Finally, and ashamedly, during my pregnancy, I harbored the secret fear that Cal might love our baby more than he loved me. I ruminated on Cal's and my walk in the park. Maybe he'd been fearful because he sensed that a switch would flip inside him on the baby's arrival. I felt the constant pulse of a low-level dread, wondering what I would do if that turned out to be the case. He wouldn't have to tell me. I would know. I would know the same way I knew when I first sniffed him out.

I was, again, wrong. When they lifted my daughter over my head (an emergency C-section after twenty-two hours of labor—don't ask), she looked down at me with her globelike eyes, and I breathed: *This is the person I have been waiting my entire life to meet.* The *exact* person. It was an instant, molecular transformation. I'd been agnostic my whole life, but in the moment of my daughter's birth, I understood Mary. After they took little Zanny out of sight to weigh her under the warming lamp, Cal looked at me, panicked: Should he stay with me? Should he go to the baby? *Go to her!* I pleaded. *Go talk to her—make sure she knows she's not alone!* He did. The fear that Cal might love the babies more than me vanished. Neither of us would ever love anyone more than we loved our babies.

———

Some women report that their partners feel neglected or even jealous when the baby is born. What happened to hanging out with friends, tossing back the martini flavor-of-the-moment? What happened to watching Jim Jarmusch or Chris Farley movies until one in the morning? Moreover, what happened to the time you used to fawn over *me* and how funny and cool *I* was? And what happened to how funny and cool *you* were? Most important, where is the sex? All understandable. None of it Cal. Many studies issued on Generation X dads report that while they're the most involved of any in American history, and help around the house more than their forefathers, they still offload the bulk of domestic burdens to women.* Cal was the classic curve thrower. We never even discussed whether he would wake up in the middle of the night with me, change diapers, any of that stuff. If he could have figured out a way to lactate, he'd have done it in a heartbeat. But he did everything else. He did the grocery shopping and cooking; he wanted to bathe, diaper, and dress Zanny; he managed the mail; I handed over my money and he paid the bills; he made the phone calls and booked the appointments; if Zanny cried, Cal wanted to console her.

When Zanny was eight weeks old, I took my first stroll without Cal to hang out in the park with an old college friend who had a three-year-old and a newborn. How was Cal taking to fatherhood, she wanted to know. Kind of amazingly, I said, ticking off everything he'd taken on, unbidden. "If I wasn't breastfeeding, I don't think she would know which one of us was the mother," I said. My friend looked at me. "Make sure he doesn't get too good at it," she said. "You're the mother." I bristled. Yuck—what a weird, sexist thing to say! Plus, for a child to feel this kind of ambidextrous attachment to her parents was, I felt, a kind of ideal. Oh, well—her issue. It probably sounded obnoxious and braggy of me to tout his bona fides. Cal's

---

* Andrew Singleton, et al., "The 'New Man' Is in the House: Young Men, Social Change, and Housework," *The Journal of Men's Studies*, vol. 12, 2004.

and my relationship, I told myself in a tone of superiority, had always been different from our friends'.

When the NASDAQ crashed just before Zanny was born, our combined income tanked along with the markets, since both our jobs were tied to the tech economy. To cut back on overhead, Cal rejiggered his business—the company he'd worked like a dog to get off the ground throughout the mid-nineties—and closed his downtown offices to work from home. True, he was making half what he'd made before, but we actually viewed it as a backhanded blessing because it meant we would both have more time to hang out with our baby.

Our baby! When she was awake, we talked to her and played with her and sang to her. When she was napping, we talked about what she had done while she was awake. When we were all asleep, we dreamed about her. Cal woke up one morning and excitedly related a dream in which she was a physicist and a runway model. *What did she look like?* I asked. He looked at me, perplexed. *What do you mean? She looked like herself, just tall.* That adorably batty response underscored a seismic shift in our sense of time and space. There was no future or past—there was no moment but the moment. In fact, life before her felt like a counterfeit existence, a way to pass the time until she was ready to come to us. One evening, I tried to introduce a thread of reflection. *What do you think of everything?* He lay back on the sofa and closed his eyes. Finally, he said: *Everything is different now.*

Everything *was* different now. Cal's prediction that day in the park was beginning to materialize—but so, I thought, was mine. This new reality, for me, called up a particular combination of love and terror. As open and wonderful as the world had become with my child's presence, it was simultaneously more treacherous than I ever could have imagined. My nearly unmanageable love for my baby made me almost frantic. Even considering that she might somehow be taken from me by the forces of nature or fate was unfathomable. I was so insanely attached to Zanny that I couldn't let anyone other than Cal take care of her for nearly a year. I knew it was crazy. I knew *I* was crazy. But picturing someone taking her away from me even into the next room—never mind out of the apartment—sent waves of pure white fear whipping up my spine. It wasn't until she was a few months old that it dawned on me that when the pediatrician and the books referred to "separation anxiety," it was meant to describe the baby's psyche, not mine.

I knew that there was no way I would be able to leave her to go into an office; my neurosis would flower into a full-blown psychotic lifestyle. This realization snapped into stark relief when Zanny was three months old. I got a call from a producer at a major television network who was revamping one of the flagship news shows; he asked if I was interested in a position as an anchor. At the time, I had already resigned from my full-time job and was freelancing, doing the kind of writing a person can do while babies nap. I certainly wasn't back to anything resembling a twelve-hour workday. I had neither employed nor made plans to employ a nanny or day-care center. As the producer described the job, I became aware, in almost an out-of-body kind of way, that had I been listening to this just three months earlier, my only challenge would have been to keep quiet until he had finished talking so that I could chirrup, "Yes! Yes! Yes!" like Molly Bloom at a job interview. But now, everything was different. It didn't sound like a great job at all, or at least it didn't sound as though taking that job would equal a great *life*. It sounded like the kind of exciting and exhausting work I'd done for fifteen years, albeit played out on the stage of national prime-time television. Which meant that I would be working a million hours a day. I looked down at my sleeping bunny rabbit. And I said no. Instead, I ramped up my freelance work—and later, got my first book deal—so that I could work from home.

Boring—to loll around with a baby all day long? Are you nuts?

The only question was why no one had told me about this sooner. I would lie in bed next to my firstborn as a newborn, watching the slide show of expressions flash across her tiny, mouselike face—the bursting of the unalloyed grin now flattening back into the neutral poker face now curling into the sad lip look—and literally ache with love. (You can hear veteran moms in my neighborhood invoke the weirdly perfect take on this kind of baby passion: "That baby is so cute it makes my uterus hurt!") I loved nursing her, nuzzling her little butternut-squash body, annoying her with spongy kisses, slurping in that sweet ricotta breath. I loved singing to her and dancing with her around our tiny living room in our rental apartment in Brooklyn, once a flop pad only for passing out after the zillion-hour workweek, or for hosting the occasional debauched party. Had I really ever smoked cartons of American Spirits, drunk bottles of wine, bent in agony over my computer, obsessively watched *Freaks and Geeks* with Cal over the nightly deliveries of Thai food, yakked on the phone until the wee hours with friends in West Coast time zones, blasted Portishead and Hole in *this* place—for *eight years*? Here, in this gentle nest of sweetness and light? It all looked the same, but I was somehow occupying a completely different space. My brain, along with our apartment, had evidently been transported to another dimension, as if some cosmic blueprint outlining the Meaning of Life had suddenly been overlaid on us.

It sounds psychedelically grandiose, like some kind of hippie awakening. Trust me, it was not. For my people, mind-expanding experiences were what you made fun of. Reality was not, as the dumb-ass sixties saying went, "a crutch for people who can't handle drugs"; our drug-doing revolved around numbing ourselves, killing pain. Reality was definitely real, it sucked, and you got mad or sad, but mostly you made poisonous, snickery comments and drove around aimlessly under the miasma of someone's mom's tranquilizers. Yet here I was, with my infant daughter, light-years away from the forces of irony. Just being with her, and watching what she was doing or "saying," forced me to see a radically different world.

There's nothing like having a baby to compel you to apply, in astonishingly literal terms, the substance of Philosophy 101. When you observe your newborn child working every waking moment to assemble a picture of you, of her own body, of the world, it makes you cringe to recall all those sophomoric conversations you—gesticulating with your hand-rolled cigarette—had with your friends about Descartes, Kant, the Platonic precept of how one comes to know the "Other." *This* is where it all happens—with infants—and it is unfolding in front of your eyes. If it is true that perception is reality, as Buddhism and quantum physics tell us, this is when the perceptual foundation is laid.

Which made me think. If you've read your Chomsky, you're acquainted with the idea that all social or cultural messages are constructed, and are invariably constructed by someone or something with a vested interest in controlling their content as well as your consumption of that content. Even if you haven't read your Chomsky, you've seen *The Matrix,* which is kind of the same thing. *Jesus,* I began thinking, *what if my perception has been wrong all along, or mostly wrong, and all I'm doing is guiding her within the confines of my fraudulent perception?* All the abstract angst I'd harbored in relation to my own upbringing lurched from the realm of the caustic joke into that of the stunningly serious, and consequently the premises of all my defensive tactics suddenly turned on me as questions that I had to answer *now*—or risk botching my own child's sense of security.

And the questions came in rapid fire. What if it is not true that your work is what you are, that it can help to dissolve the psychic weight of your hideous adolescence? Moreover, what if the whole way I was raised was wrong, and that whole excuse for having had a shitty childhood—"You were raised like that, and *you* turned out okay"—was the biggest load of crap of all time? What if I was *not* okay? In fact, the more I thought about it, the more I began to think that while I might be okay at this very moment, I had not turned out okay at all in the scheme of things. I *had* become a pretty fucked-up adult. I'd gorged myself maudlin and frantic on drugs and booze for more than a decade. I'd spent my teens as a punky truant running myself and boyfriends ragged, my twenties as a workaholic drama queen running myself and Cal ragged. Maybe now, at the threshold of my thirties as a sober married woman and mom, it was time to sort through the whole messy hill of beans. Maybe I *was* a slave: born into bondage, into a prison that I couldn't taste or see or touch, a prison for my *mind*. Dude. The red pill—give it.

I had always thought that at least my infancy and early childhood were decent, but the more I thought about it now, the more scandalized I was. There was no *way* I was going to hand Zanny off to a bunch of babysitters—what if they were like Hilary, or worse, like Bonnie, the evil fairy-tale queen? No *way* was I going to read her the damn *Highwayman* as a *bedtime* story—I was going to read her comforting, sweet stories and listen to her *feelings*! And what *non-thought*s were going through my parents' minds when they decided that it was *okay* for my dad to go *ice climbing* with an *infant*? Mother of *God*! That photo was banished to storage.

Listening to stories about my own babyhood now became all but intolerable. The casual abuse! The banality of evil! "We were just following doctor's orders." Averting her eyes in a dramatic way—but in a way transparently calculated to look as though it was not dramatic—my mother commented to me one day as I was nursing Zanny that I had been "allergic" to her breast milk.

"What in the world can you be talking about?" I sputtered. "That's the craziest thing I've ever heard!"

"Well, it may sound crazy to *you*, but my doctor at the *French Hospital* of San Francisco said that in very rare cases, a baby is simply *unable* to digest her mother's . . . milk . . . and that you were *clearly* one of these children," my mother sniffed. "You were a very allergic child, *extremely* colicky."

Silence. I stared at her.

"Well, the baby will be able to start taking solid food soon, in any case," my mother then declared, changing the subject to what she must have thought was a less controversial topic. Wrong. Solid food! What could she be talking about now? Was she out of her mind? Babies should have nothing but breast milk until they're at least six months old! Nothing but! At least! And then they still need to be nursed for at least a year!

"Six *months* old!" My mother was aghast. "Why, you were six *weeks* old when you started eating applesauce!" I felt the blood drop out of my brain. Six weeks. A baby is barely able to lift her head at that age, never mind digest solid food. No wonder I was "colicky." Had she been trying to kill me?

"Well, things may be different now, but I do know one thing *absolutely*," my mother retorted. "You *adored* applesauce."

A year and change later, when Zanny started uttering her first words, I asked my mom what my first word had been.

"Well, I don't know that I want to tell you," she said, after a belabored pause on her end of the phone line.

"Stop with the Brontë theatrics," I said, annoyed. "Just tell me like a regular mother."

"Well, you're *not* going to like it, my dear," she said, threateningly.

"What *was* it?"

" 'Scotch'! All right? It was 'scotch.' "

Silence.

"Well, I *told* you that you wouldn't like it," she said, satisfied, a glass clinking in the background.

When I relate this story to people ten years younger, Generation Y, they are properly horrified. This is the generation whose parents fawned over them, giving everyone a blue ribbon whether they had come in first, second, or third place—or any place. They love their parents! They have said so, in public, for nearly a decade now, making such perky declarations to the press in stories about generational differences as "my parents are my best friends!" It is also the generation that is such a well-documented pain in the ass in the workplace because they expect everyone older than they to tell them what an amazing job they're doing with every office memo they staple together. When I tell this story to friends my own age, however, they cackle with conspiratorial delight. "Oh my God," they say. "That is so fucking *great*." Then, after we stop giggling, there is a moment. We push the strollers silently. And then someone says to the kids, "Hey! Who wants a Tofutti ice-cream sandwich?"

As phenomenally delicious as having children often is, it can also be phenomenally sad for Xers. The old truism about finally being able to understand, and sympathize with, your parents and their choices after you have your own children often just doesn't hold up for many of us. Rather, we find ourselves wondering how our parents could have acted the way they did. Cal, though one of the few, was not the only person my age with a good relationship with his still-married parents. I do have some friends who not only had none of these childhood issues with their parents, but also remain on excellent terms with them. I love hearing stories of their upbringing much in the same way that I like to read books like *Eat, Pray, Love* or *A Year in Provence,* whose narratives recount life experiences so remote from my own financial and familial circumstances that they function as refreshing weekend trips to virtual reality. But even more, I love seeing those friends with their parents now because it gives me the idea that it might be possible to have this kind of relationship with my own children when they are grown.

Take my friend "Holly," for example. The eldest of three, Holly grew up in a solid middle-class home with a smart stay-at-home mother and a stable, no-frills, fishing kind of dad. Her complaints about her parents are that they are kind of provincial; her mom can be casually stinging, and her dad, she says, is relatively boring and unimaginative. But the basic point is: *So?* I've known Holly for twenty years, and her position on her parents has never varied: She loves them and is grateful for her happy, normal childhood. Holly and her siblings went on to attend prestigious colleges and graduate schools; they became experts in American Modernism, opera, and neurobiology; they have traveled to interesting places and have had complicated, grown-up relationships. Holly's adult life is nothing like her parents'. She is a single mother living in New York City and working on the highly competitive, ridiculously overeducated sales force of a high-end antiques dealer. But what makes Holly a freak by our generation's standards is that instead of resenting or comparing the differences in their lives, she has renewed admiration and appreciation for her mom's graceful management of the daily needs of three children, essentially single-handed. Holly's mom, as ever, is a source of genuine comfort, support, and inspiration to her. In fact, in talking about the demise of her own marriage, Holly often reflects that her upbringing is to blame only in that it is hard to find a mate whose own background matches the stability of her own. "Most of the men I'm attracted to are complex and interesting—which I love and want—but they have these tortured interior lives because of their childhoods," she says. "Basically, I'm not that emotionally complicated because my childhood was, well, good. It is impossible for me to understand what it is like to live so constantly with such demons."

Imagine what it would be like to inhabit Holly's clear, peaceful psyche! Those demons, for people like me, have been sitting on our shoulders since the mists of early childhood began burning off in adolescence, which makes us available to lecture to our minority peers like Holly about their ethnographic patterns. But obviously we can't understand Holly's relationship to her parents any more than she can understand ours. Holly *wants* child-rearing advice from her mother because she *trusts* her. Holly's own mother *is* her model "Mom." When people like Holly encounter a food ad with the words "homemade—just like Mom used to make!" they think: "Yum!" For people like me, though, that same gee-whillikers cheer makes something inside us snicker and sink at the same rate. We want to be that mom, but we don't know the first thing about her. Often, instead, we start by deciding what kind of mom we *don't* want to be.

As much as I admired my own mom, it was clear to me from the get-go that she and I would not occupy the same segment of the mother continuum. Take, for example, sleep. Other than breast-feeding, sleep ranks as the top point of concern for first-time parents of newborns. After the first month or so, many parents begin to start sniffing out the fallacy of their own parents' recollections whenever they're offered as counterpoint to the current state of nighttime affairs: "Well, goodness, honey, we just laid you down, and *you* went right to sleep—*you* never fussed." One can only guess how many Gen-X parents around the country who have been sucker-punched out of sleep for the fifth time that night wonder, while trying yet another strategy that might soothe their little biscuit back to sleep: *Really?* That's *really* how it went, Mom? Amy, a Louisiana-native friend whom I met when her four boys were all under five years old—and who is every bit the bright-eyed, yes-we-can, ass-kicking mom (the kind who, irritatingly, always seems to have extra organic snacks at the playground for *your* children, too)—snorts at such reconstructive memories. "I've never heard of a baby who just *falls asleep,*" she snaps. "What were they giving us? Dramamine? Benadryl? Bourbon?" No comment.

What Amy did is what so many other X parents have done: used the cribs as laundry hampers, bought a king-sized mattress, flopped it on the floor, and piled everyone on. This sleeping arrangement, called "the family bed" or "co-sleeping," was popularized by William Sears, M.D., the leading attachment-parenting pediatrician and Generation X's Dr. Spock. The co-sleeping setup means that you keep the babies and toddlers in bed with you so that you can nurse them down to sleep and throughout the night, cuddle them if they wake up, and just generally mammal them up. In X territory, the family bed presents as a highly contentious issue, and not necessarily because the American Association of Pediatrics strongly advises against it on account of suffocation concerns. Ask new X parents, and they'll likely tell you that yes, though they've had some of the weirdest, fraught encounters of their lives with other parents over the family bed, pro or con, people rarely brought up suffocation as the chief source of distress (that's the domain of the grandparents, who send frantic emails citing various studies).

Although there are those who sit in the middle, most people, particularly mothers, are apt to be in one camp or the other. One woman whom I barely knew at the time, for example, made it her mission to convince me not only that I was wrong to do the family bed thing, but that I was also actively damaging my children and family life. I can't remember how she found out about our sleep setup, but she was positively implacable on the subject and harassed me every time I saw her, which was daily since our children went to the same preschool. On the other end of the continuum, another woman—also a relative stranger at the time—confided in me outright that she felt that people who "forced" their children to sleep alone were like Nazis—not in the inappropriately casual, lowercase way in which people often invoke the term. She meant the actual proper noun "Nazis."

Here's the thing: If one wishes to trace the primal legacy of *on their own floor, crying alone,* one need look no further than the family bed. Or at least that was the thing for me. I heard the con arguments: that there is no lasting damage from forcing babies to cry it out at night, that they need to learn how to soothe themselves, that they don't remember it anyway, that you need *your* sleep. Totally got it. But having unplugged from my own matrix, my feeling was: Not on my watch. The goal of the crying-it-out method seemed to me, at root, to instill a form of Pavlovian "learned helplessness" in which babies would learn that no matter what they did to summon help, no help would come. So how would one conduct a longitudinal study that would prove that there is no lasting damage from this? What would be the adult echo of infant self-soothing? How about booze, smokes, drugs, and crippling codependence? I remembered many nights as a child jolting awake from a nightmare, alone in the dark, and becoming so riven with fear that I was virtually chloroformed back to unconsciousness by it; I remembered Ian, clutching his elephant stuffie, deserted in his cold room. I didn't mind what anyone else wanted to do, but I wasn't taking any chances with the crying-it-out thing. And since neither Cal nor I did drugs or drank anymore, rolling over wasn't a big concern. Moreover, it is said that a nursing mother has a somatic sense that remains alert to the infant beside her, and I found that to be the case. Another perk was that it allowed the baby and me to stay mostly asleep all night; instead of everyone having to wake up in a panic every few hours to nurse, I could just roll over, like a dog mama, and let her latch on. It worked for Cal because he grew up in a culture that talks a good game about the dangers of "spoiling" babies and young children but is, in fact, one of the mushiest, cuddliest baby-spoiling societies in the world.

The family bed also worked because neither Cal nor I was interested in sex. We didn't scuff around it awkwardly, as had been our custom; it didn't even come up. Weirdly, my mother was the only one who hinted at it. "Aren't there certain conjugal . . . matters . . . that might emerge?" she asked. *What?* It was the first time my mother had ever acknowledged that sex existed, other than the official conversation that had ambushed me at bedtime one night when I was five years old (after which my only question had been: "Have you told Uncle Emmett about this?"). "*No,* there are *not,*" I snapped. And thank you for suddenly making it your business now. Cal and I were on the same page about full-time babysitters, too. Whereas my mother's motto had been "One can't pay enough for good help," Cal's had been "You can't trust anyone but your family!" Every household was populated by aunties, uncles, grandparents, cousins; there was always someone to watch the children. Children always went to the grown-up parties, and in fact, there were no grown-up parties; all parties were for families. Getting tired, *ning?* Take a nap under the mah-jongg table!

But for all the focus that his upbringing had trained on families, Cal had not felt as though a great deal of attention was paid to children, at least not insofar as their individual needs and personalities went. Be a doctor! That was the extent of the guidance, and the guidance was harsh and unvarying. Moreover, as stated, he had always felt like an outsider, not just in the company of Americans but in his own family; they didn't really understand him. Marveling at our instinctive attention to our children, Cal reflected on his own childhood. "I wish someone had done for *me* what we're doing for the kids," he said. "I never knew what I was, or what I wanted to do. Until now, really." In fatherhood, Cal was seeing who he was for the first time. Just as the wedding star chart had predicted.

But what he was finding was different from what many fathers find. Usually dads, even Gen-X dads, are a little more casual about child rearing. Fathers are credited, historically and psychologically, with bringing the outside world and its values into the home. Naturally, as social conditions have evolved to produce a generalized equality of the sexes, so have the specific dad job requirements, but the fundamentals still persist. Psychology texts inform us that the relative esteem in which the father holds his children directly affects their sense of status and worth at large. For example, dads are more likely than moms to roughhouse and, in so doing, teach children about appropriate aggression, self-defense, the limits of fair play. Dads are more likely than moms to encourage risk taking, which helps impress on children the particular contours of their prowess, as well as simple grit. Because dads don't typically sweat the small stuff, they let kids see that a little rule relaxing won't collapse the whole system. My own dad, when the good twin aspect of his Gemini dichotomy was activated, had been this way when I was little. My dad, now that Zanny was here, was essentially AWOL. Cal wasn't surprised. But I actually was. Before I had had the babies, my dad had noodged me about it. "So, when are we going to see little Jasper or Jarvis running around the old Thomas place, Suze?" he might let drop during the rare phone call. Or the more inscrutable: "Better step it up there, little darlin', before the Ancient One progresses further into the dark of night." Huh? It was weird. I'd be thinking: *Why would you care about my having children when you barely make time to call me?* But at the same time, I noted, and filed, such comments. Dad loved babies and little kids; he had been a perfect father when I was little. Maybe he was waiting for the reprise. I held out hope, albeit on a long and tenuous rope.

The rope snapped soon after Zanny was born. Dad showed up at the hospital (drunk, I later found out), but his interest waned almost instantly. Wild with excitement and glee, I had sent him updates and albums; they landed in the void. On September 11, 2001, I watched the twin towers collapsing into dust from our kitchen window, clutching five-month-old Zanny. This was before Cal started working from home, and his office had been about ten blocks away from Ground Zero. But my deadline for an article had forced him to stay home just late enough to escape being at work at the moment of impact. With the phone lines down or jammed, my mother and Joseph sent frantic emails and chat messages every five minutes to see if we were okay; hours later, calls and messages from friends I hadn't seen in years poured in; an English couple that Cal and I had met briefly on our honeymoon tracked us down from their country home in northern France. My father? Nothing. I finally called him a week later, trembling. *Just wanted to let you know that we're not dead,* I said. Silence. *Well,* he said. *Glad to hear it.*

I squeezed my Zanny and kissed her fuzzy baby head: Here was his granddaughter, his only grandchild. I had little reason to sustain connection with him after that.

Cal occupied the pole diametrically opposite my father. He watched Zanny's every action and reaction as closely as I did. In fact, he was downright noodgy, but I didn't mind; he was the most adoring, attentive parent I'd ever seen. He worried that she wasn't comfortable ("This onesie *sucks*! I'm tossing it!"); that certain positions made her unhappy ("She doesn't like that hold—you have to hold her like *this,* or she gets upset"); that certain foods were too difficult for her to digest or that she just didn't like them ("It wasn't that stomach bug—it was the avocado you gave her, seriously"); that the toys we had were not sufficient to stimulate her development ("This is the worst goddamned shape-sorter I've ever seen—who gave this to her?"). We had mainly lived on takeout during our pre-baby years together, and while that continued during our collective postpartum period, all that changed once Zanny started eating solid food. Cal took over the kitchen. He loved cooking; he had always been better at it than I was. I lined up more work; I was better at juggling than he was. We were a great team, I thought.

Again, our setup drew concern from the grandparent section. How *wonderful* that I had taken so *powerfully* to motherhood, my mother said—and how *miraculous* Cal's devotion to fatherhood was! What a lucky baby Zanny was to have *two* such *adoring* parents! Now, don't attack her just *yet,* as she simply wished to ask the *question:* Were we *really* going to be able to get anything *done?* Were we *certain* that we didn't need a babysitter? Couldn't we ask around for the name of a good service? *She* had always found a good service *invaluable;* it would only provide the most *qualified* applicants. No thanks, we said; we're good. For her part, Cal's mother was flat-out apoplectic. What kind of a *man* was her son, working from *home?* *And* cooking and changing *diapers?* He was a *house-husband,* that's what! Why wasn't he out finding a *job,* to provide for his *family?* He was not *ambitious*! He was *lazy*! Why wasn't *the mother* (me) taking care of the house?

These reproaches were enraging, and it felt as if all the goodwill that Cal's mother and I had stitched up over the years was getting yanked out at the seams. "So, it's more important to her to uphold some dumb-ass, retrograde idea of manhood than it is for you to be a good father?" I would rail. Cal shrugged. "That's how she is—you can't do anything about it," he'd say. "Plus, it's guilt talking because she knows that's how she raised me." It was true: She had basically raised Cal to be a housewife. Just as it is true that the easiest way to discover whatever is unhealed from your childhood is to have children, it is true that you can learn what was good about your childhood by having children; you find yourself bucking the former and reflexively enacting the latter. Cal had loved tending house as a child, so he was doing it now that he had a child. He was more than good at it, he was *perfect*.

So? So *what* if some facets of traditional gender roles were topsy-turvy in our new family? Wasn't that what the women's movement had fought to encourage—the empowered woman, the feminized man? Wasn't this what our generation was *supposed* to be doing? Moreover, by working from home and raising our child ourselves, weren't we not only offering our daughter egalitarian role models, but also avoiding the cycle of exploiting immigrant mothers who worked as nannies to send money back to their own children abroad? What part of the way in which Cal and I were raising our child was not an obvious reflection of having it all? *Whatever*, parents! We were going to do things our way. *Everything is different now.*

I wonder, as I step back to survey all of us as peers, if there has ever been a more defensive generation of parents. When I asked for her reflections on the subject, my in every way excellent pediatrician, Philippa Gordon, told me that she routinely sees X parents "ferociously advocating for their children, responding with hostility to anyone they perceive as getting in the child's way—from a person whose dog snuffles inquiringly at a baby in a carriage, to a teacher or coach who they perceive is slighting their child, to a poor hapless doctor who cannot cure the common cold." What she seemed to be saying is that X parents somehow have developed the idea that their children cannot handle reality. It's as though we're subjecting them to the emotional corollary of everyone's favorite Travolta teen beat classic, *The Boy in the Plastic Bubble*. "There is a feeling," Dr. Gordon went on to say, "that anything interfering with their kid's homeostasis, as they see it, is an inappropriate behavior to be fended off sharply."

I giggled sheepishly on hearing this, recalling the first time Cal and I took Zanny to the park. It was a fabulously gorgeous spring day: People were out biking, kite-flying in the meadow, having picnics. As Cal and I huddled around our six-week-old baby girl, who was lying comfortably on a blanket and contentedly gazing up at a cherry tree, I glared out at the scene: What the fuck were people thinking, playing *Frisbee*? Didn't this strike anyone as *dangerous*? Why were so many dogs unleashed, just galloping around wherever? And what about all these *bees*? This whole situation struck me as a death trap, a suicide rap. Within fifteen minutes, we packed up, outraged. When, a few weeks later, I confessed this park incident to my first real mom friend, Genina, she shared with me that as she had been strolling her newborn son, Sam, an acorn had dropped from a tree and pegged the top of the stroller, triggering her reflexive primal shriek, "What the hell is your problem?" Addressed to the tree.

Whatever your take on our parental forebears may be, you can say with confidence that they were not screaming at bees and trees to back off from their children. They were, experts say, more concerned about their children's behavior toward others than the other way around. But this state of psychic affairs may also highlight what makes X tick, as a group—specifically, a reaction to how they themselves grew up. When I spoke about this to the child psychiatrist and a chair of the American Academy of Child and Adolescent Psychiatry Dr. Michael Brody, he said simply: "You all are doing what all parents do: trying to heal the wounds from your own childhoods through your children." Yup. Given this, is it really all that surprising that we've become attachment-parenting zealots—that Baby Boomers accuse us of being family values neocons, Eisenhower Era throwbacks? In trying to protect our children from experiencing the kind of anxiety and neglect that we suffered as kids, we are apparently not being able to separate our own feelings from our children's.

"Generation X parents seem to have mistaken emotional 'enmeshment' for 'attachment parenting,' " Brody pointed out.

It's a really good point, and I totally get it. But what can you do? As a new parent, I couldn't help feeling—still can't, albeit to a lesser extent now that my two older children are school-aged—that I would rather hurl myself in front of a bus than for my kiddos to get their feelings hurt. Naturally, people who don't have children, as well as older generations, all respond with variations on the theme "You can't protect them from everything, and it's not healthy or even right to try." To this I again say, yup—and anyone with any cranial twitch fiber knows that what you say is true. But knowing that never seems to change my feelings, and judging from my peers' comparably cognitive dissonant behavior, it's the same story for them. Self-awareness doesn't necessarily seem to be an effective salve. We can self-dissect—even self-eviscerate—to our snarky, laden hearts' content, but *The Drama of the Gifted Child* reminds us, like the monster in the closet, that we "continue to live in [our] repressed childhood situation, ignoring the fact that it no longer exists." *

No news flash here. Over the past several years, it has become well established in the popular press that X parents are overprotective, overinvolved—overattached, some might say. In 2005, journalist Judith Warner's bestselling polemic *Perfect Madness: Motherhood in the Age of Anxiety* skewered the rise of upper-middle-class, post-feminist mothering for its obsessive perfectionism about raising developmentally correct children (as well as American public policy for neglecting to support families). Part of what inspired me to write my own first book, *Buy, Buy Baby: How Consumer Culture Manipulates Parents and Harms Young Minds,* was having investigated in an article the marketing industry's exploitation of Generation X's attachment neuroses. Further reporting for the book on my generation's mania as I was raising two children under the age of three made for a mind-blowing revelation, compelling me to look more

* Miller, p. 2.

deeply at what was triggering my consumer behavior as well as my parenting decisions. Not that I could change the instincts, though I thought it was important to look more analytically at the consumption reflexes.

Even established advocates of attachment parenting have started saying "Enough already." In 2007, less than a decade after publishing the seminal book on the advantages of attachment parenting, the author Katie Allison Granju wrote an invective for the hip parenting site Babble.com arguing that Gen X mothers had supplanted postwar homemaker concerns with postfeminist neuroses about child development. She called this phenomenon an "over-parenting crisis," going so far as to characterize its reach as "epidemic." It's not that Granju had changed her mind about attachment parenting. Rather, the issue had become, in a way, one of quantity, not quality. "In our hyperfocus on all things parenting," she wrote, "are we bungling the very thing we seek to perfect?"

It's a ridiculously complicated question for us to answer. But it's pretty clear what everyone else thinks. When it got to the point, as it did in 2005, that a local barkeep felt compelled to post a "Stroller Manifesto"—the now infamous public remonstrance of overattached parents in Park Slope, begging them to get a freaking babysitter instead of rolling up, en masse, to happy hour with their howling infants and toddlers—clearly the weight of the zeitgeist had gotten to the bone-crushing stage. Even those who vowed to revile X's "the-world-is-my-changing-table" philosophy when their baby time came, now find themselves somehow insidiously absorbed into the machine. The *New York* magazine sex columnist turned wife and mother Amy Sohn bemoaned her own *et tu?* moment a few years ago. Who is it we're afraid to leave alone—the babies or ourselves? In spite of vowing never to be one of those annoying Stroller Manifesto addressees, she found herself with fellow infant-strapped parents making a family-style nuisance out of herself at a trendy Brooklyn restaurant. "We had," she wrote, "become Them."

But X seems to take special pleasure in cataloging in epic detail the ways in which we suck. Remember that scene in *8 Mile* where Eminem wins the battle before the other guy even gets onstage, by preemptively using the competition's ammunition against himself? We're all like that. We're all the real Slim Shady. We'll tell you all about our legion faults and shortcomings—more than, perhaps, you cared to know—well before your finger curls around the trigger. (Contrast with Baby Boomers' protest-era megaphone-style self-promotion: The Whole World Is Watching! The Revolution Will Be Televised! Stand and Deliver! Don't Stop Thinking About Tomorrow!) You would think that such excruciating self-analysis would count for something psychologically, and it does, so far as our generation's contributions to entertainment and media are concerned. But where parenting is concerned, excruciating self-analysis seems to get you only so far. It certainly doesn't seem to keep you from acting like an asshole, any more than knowing about his whole prophecy kept Oedipus from killing his father and schtupping his mother. For one thing, our attempts to reconcile our own childhood wounds in parenthood yields some very odd, pop-culty results that peg us as sandwich-board-wearing chumps.

Indeed, we're such obvious targets that you can see us from the Washington desk of the *New York Times* columnist, smug Bobo Boomer, and self-described "comic sociologist," David Brooks, who observed back in 2007 that Park Slope mothers—by making mini-me's of their infants, dressing them in Ramones onesies and skull-and-crossbones booties—were offending those who understood that babies had a right to be babies. Say what you will about Brooks, but he was totally right. Please. We could all add enough of our own weird, sorry examples to pack what's left of the Staten Island landfill. For instance, what did I do when I wanted to talk to my children about racism? I blasted Public Enemy's "911's a Joke." My children and I then discussed how justifiably upset and angry the people singing the song were when the police wouldn't come because they weren't considered important enough to help, which spurred a fascinating conversation. I can hear Brooks clearing his throat contemptuously. My six-year-old's favorite song, at last check, was "Spanish Bombs"; my nine-year-old's is "Life on Mars?" and just the other day I caught myself cooing the bing-bong part of "Satellite of Love" to my newborn son. I know, Brooks, I know who I am, and I'm not proud. But I'll see you *and* I'll raise you. My sandwich board reads ALL APOLOGIES! You can see it from the numbing, frigid desert of deep space.

X parents also brook a lot of bad behavior in our children, even though we may not consciously think that we do. As an Xer, you may feel great sympathy for people's complaints that our well-attached kids are, well, rude. You may hear outrageous stories, like the 2009 post I read on a *New York Times* blog recounting a preschooler's purposely tripping a woman in a crowded restaurant and chortling, " 'Mommy, did you see me trip that woman? I tripped her!' " with no corrective measure from the mother. You may join a grandmother in her mortification when she asks for advice on Grandparents.com on how to handle her grandson's relentless public insulting of his own mother, who seems unable—or unwilling—to stand up to such mistreatment. You can even understand that indulging this kind of rudeness can have more serious behavioral consequences for your young children down the line. As a 2005 Yale study revealed, preschool students are expelled at a rate more than three times that of children in grades K–12 because of behavioral problems. Preschoolers? God only knows how our kids will get jobs if they're getting kicked out of preschool.

But you don't need to read that kind of stuff in studies or on blogs to know that it's as true as it is crazy. Because you sense an uncomfortable cognitive dissonance in your own psyche, you know that you're somehow part of the problem. You also really don't need to ask child development experts for affirmation, but what the experts have to say is: Yes, today's kids are ruder than ever, and it is the fault of the generation that's raising them. Which is to say, us. The consensus is that we, in general, are so fixated on our children's emotional well-being that we may be teaching them that everyone else's feelings are comparatively unimportant—a poor etiquette twist on the Nirvana chorus "All alone is all we are."

What Brooks and his Boomer sympathizers dismiss as pathetic vanity is of course more than that. But it nonethless raises bizarre, vaguely troubling questions about us as parents. Why do we outfit our infants in "Koo-Koo for Cocoa Puffs" and "Silly Rabbit! Trix Are for Kids!" onesies, but feed them homemade organic baby food and breast-feed them way past their first birthdays? Why are we all so drawn to caustic parodies of the Saturday morning cartoons of our childhood on late-night TV? Why do we have such dissonant responses to wholesomeness and cheesiness? Are we trying as adults to normalize the icky, sexualized, psychedelic gestalt of the media and culture that came in through the front door while our parents weren't watching?

Yes, we are. Still, I'm not convinced that this is all bad. I know that I continually walk the line that divides attachment parenting and enmeshment parenting because of my childhood neuroses. But it can be instructive. Take, for instance, the Princess Game.

When Zanny was three years old, the girls in her preschool developed a circle that revolved around the Disney princesses. Anyone who wasn't wearing a dress of the trademarked hue of the princess of the day wasn't allowed to join in the game, so if you weren't wearing powder blue on Cinderella day, you were out. For starters, my daughter had only the barest notion of who Cinderella, Snow White, and the rest of them were, even in their original fairy-tale configurations, since I had felt that she was far too young to hear such scary stories. I agree with Bruno Bettelheim and the raft of other child development experts who argue that these folk archetypes help little ones work through their primal fears of parental abandonment and so forth, but as they will tell you, children aren't ready for this kind of psychic challenge until they are five or six. On the basis of such thinking, I'd decided to wait with the whole Brothers Grimm oeuvre until she reached kindergarten. Moreover, as you might expect from the author of a book on early childhood and consumerism, I had made our home a no-Disney zone, so my daughter was not acquainted with the princesses' merchandising sorority. This meant that, faced with the Princess Game at the age of three, my little schmushkie was confused, excluded, scared by stories she didn't understand, and hurt.

By the time I had actually pieced together what was going on by picking up the fragments that Zanny offered, asking teachers what she might be talking about, and then running such patched-together snippets by the other mothers for their take, I was beside myself. My daughter's tiny little self; her tender-lipped face! She had borne this thorny situation, alone, for at least two weeks. The teachers hadn't tuned in to it, in part because my daughter's modus operandi is to affect a poker face in public, particularly in the throes of stress. It didn't seem as though anything was bothering her. But it was. It was my *job* to know what was bothering her, and it had taken me two weeks to figure it out. Dropping her off at school that morning, I was vibrating at such a high pitch of anxiety that when I let go of her hand as she walked into school, I felt my skin had slipped off with it, leaving the ragged meat of my fingers pulsing in full view of my daughter, of the children, the other mothers.

I was crazed. I had to stop it. I had to stop it. What could I do? How could a Montessori school allow such social deviance and transparent marketing to intrude on early childhood education? I wanted to lecture the parents until I could feel smoke billowing from my ears: How can you let your daughters behave this way, and moreover, how can all you liberals countenance creating a new generation of sexist shopaholics? What the hell is wrong here when preschoolers are acting like queen bees and wannabes? I was racked with guilt: How could I allow my rarefied, navel-gazing notions of the walled garden of childhood to bar my little girl from simply making friends? I had done this. Then I started to despise the little girls: petty, small-minded, vicious little creatures. That's when I knew I was really nuts. *They were three years old.*

I finally summoned the courage to talk to the teachers, somehow managing to keep my shit together enough to couch my concerns diplomatically. They were not only wholly sympathetic but grateful that I had raised the issue; frankly, they hadn't noticed that the game was having such an impact on the girls, much less on stoic little Zanny. As we progressed through a really thoughtful and rich conversation, it dawned on me that this might be one of those instances in which my hypersensitivity had the capacity to be useful, much in the same way that it had fueled my determination to probe the marketing industry's targeting young children. Huh.

At home, my daughter and I talked through her feelings, which ultimately inspired us to embark on an exploration of Cinderella stories from around the world; every culture has one, and we compared the Mexican, Chinese, Caribbean, and Disney versions. She was comforted when I assured her that her teachers knew about the Princess Game and were going to help all the girls, including her, work through it at school; and they did, in a loving and thoughtful way. The game sparked heartfelt and nuanced conversation among all the mothers; I was interested in, and learned a lot from, their insights. One day, nine months later, my daughter had a friend over for a playdate. I overheard the friend say: "Hey! I thought you said you had princess costumes!" My daughter replied: "I *do* have princess costumes—they just aren't *Disney* princess costumes. Disney just wants you to *buy* all their stuff, and I just like making my own." In addition to taking sheepish pleasure in her punk-rock resistance efforts, I felt a blossoming of peace and pride: Everyone had done so well.

And, really, it would have been so easy to miss. The whole thing. Even I, in my enmeshment parenting craze, almost had. The parents I knew as a kid hadn't particularly been looking out for these things. They were so small, barely discernible: No well-adjusted person would have taken notice of them. But how many times as a child had

I found myself suddenly in the midst of confusing, scary circumstances, not understanding enough about the contours of my own feelings to know what they meant, much less the vocabulary required to speak up about them? I can't say. For my friends and me, probably the outline of our childhoods could be traced via the sequence of such moments: wandering, confused, unsafe. I wanted my own babies to feel, from the start, that the adults around them were paying attention, were there to help untangle the bramble in front of them—that we might not be able to clear it entirely, but that we were unknitting it alongside and behind them. Not alone. I did not want my children to feel alone.

But what if, in spite of our best efforts, we failed them anyway? Or, rather, what if *I* failed them? Cal, with his unalterable compass, wouldn't be capable of it. And beyond his solid upbringing, part of the reason for this, I thought, was his sense of faith—as in a holy connection. I had, to be exact, less than zero. I remember with excruciating clarity the moment I asked my mother the Death question. I was four, and I was tucked into bed under my hippie patchwork quilt with my Snoopy. My mom laid out the standard secular humanist line: No one knows, but some people believe that you go to "Heaven" (oh); others think that you die for a little while but are reborn as some other kind of thing (wha?); others are pretty sure that's *that* (what?!). And thus launched a lifetime of existential fear and nihilistic dread. What *really* happens? What really *is* God, if anything?

My commitment to trying to cultivate some, any kind of, faith had started with a question posed by Zanny a few months after she turned two. She and I were stumping up to the park on an airless summer day. She spotted a dried-up earthworm on the sidewalk and wanted to know what had happened to it. The second I said that it had died—meaning, it was not alive anymore—I knew what was next: "What happens to things when they aren't alive anymore?" Of course she wanted to know—who doesn't? Standing there dumbly, I thought, (a) you should have been rehearsing this moment since she was in utero, and (b) you have the next ten seconds to get this right.

Had I been of a different background or generation—the kind that has fixed ideas on what to say to kids—handling this perennial ontological riddle would have been a piece of cake. But I did not know how to handle it, and I didn't know many people who did, either. It does seem funny that most people my age whom I know are dumbstruck by the whole God thing and what to tell their kids. For a crop of parents so dishy and analytical about everything from nursing in front of their fathers-in-law to whether to introduce toddlers to *Star Wars* to "red-shirting" kindergartners, it seems weird that this should leave us so stumped. Then again, we are the generation that felt that everything was essentially bullshit. Then we had kids, and everything became important again. And if there was ever a decidedly no-bullshit scenario, it's talking to your little boo-boo-head about God, a Higher Power, the Afterlife—all that.

It's not that we don't want to. At least according to my own unscientific survey, most of us do want to offer our kids spiritual undergirding. But that survey also says that the spiritually confused and/or dissatisfied generally fall into one of three camps. The first are those who grew up with religion but don't feel particularly connected to the associated traditions and values. The second camp is conflicted about its religion of origin; the third never had one to begin with and is lost. The bottom line seems to be that we want it, but it has to feel *real, authentic*. But how do you *do* that? What does that even mean?

Take the case of my friend whom I'll call Simone. Simone grew up a stone's throw from the West Virginia mountains, and her hometown was traditional United Methodist. But because it was also a college town, and her dad was a professor, Simone always felt as though she got just the right mixture of skepticism and faith. She wanted the same experience for her two kids, six and four years old. But not only had her perspective broadened with adulthood, life was also different for her children than it had been for her. For one thing, she was troubled about the church split over gay marriage. For another, her kids were born in Dallas, Texas—a far cry from small-town Methodism. Moreover, Simone was divorced shortly after the birth of her second child; the women of the church were mostly married, traditional. Ditto when she moved to Jacksonville, Florida. There were uncomfortable moments, alienating periods. But Simone says that things worked themselves out because she and her church community were guided by what they'd been taught from childhood: love, tolerance, service. "It's funny," she wrote to me, "but when you're raised on an idea or concept, all the answers to the thorny questions are answered when you need them to be."

Astonishing. Same thing with the case of another friend, "Stacey." Mother of three in Glendale, California, Stacey grew up in Hawaii and was active in Protestant youth groups, even as her Catholic-born mom dabbled in Buddhism. Throughout her twenties, she herself practiced Buddhism before she decided to adopt her husband's faith, Judaism. It was the richness of Jewish family traditions—celebrating the Sabbath together every Friday night, attending temple as a family, Hebrew school for the kids—that compelled her to convert. Stacey's connection to God, Lord of the Universe, the Higher Power—all that—was already firmly entrenched in childhood.

So, my question for first- and second-campers has always been: Is it necessary for one's connection to God, and the spiritual/religious customs that one might adopt for the sake of family bonding, to be strictly intertwined? To the observant, this probably sounds like straight-up sacrilege. You can't just swap out religious tenets because you feel like it! What's the point of religion at all, then? But if erstwhile nihilistic Gen Xers turned parents do, indeed, want to include a sense of faith and tradition in the raising of kids—but need it to feel *real, authentic*—then another point is: If you believe, then it's *all* good.

In the case of Cal, this point had stuck hard, even as it backfired. A lapsed Catholic, he couldn't countenance the Church of his upbringing. At the same time, no other religious tradition felt legitimate. So when, in a fever of seeking, I ultimately found and joined an ultraprogressive Protestant church whose mission we both supported, Cal could never bring himself to go. "I know it sounds dumb, but it just doesn't feel real without the Stations of the Cross," he said. You might think that his is an extreme example of a first-category camper: someone whose faith was stripped, leaving him with only with religious trappings. But here's the interesting thing. Of all my friends and family, Cal was perhaps the most grounded in faith. In fact, when I was in my twenties and having panic attacks about life after death—wildly grasping at any answer—it was his sureness of the soul's eternal nature that quelled my terror. For him, this was shoulder-shrugging territory.

What first- and second-campers have in common is that they're bilingual, in spiritual terms. Even if they tinkered with, or scrapped, their religion of origin, they know the milieu of higher communion the way they know English and another foreign language. They can pick and choose whatever customs and traditions feel good and right for their families because their relationship with a Higher Power is already real and authentic. If I wanted real and authentic, I'd better train up. At least, that's how Martin Buber might have thought about it. Buber, if you're feeling a little rusty in the freshman philosophy department, was an Austrian-Israeli-Jewish philosopher, and his seminal work, *I and Thou,* argued that most of the time we relate to other people, things, and events in the world as "it"—that which is fundamentally outside ourselves—which he characterized as I-It relations. In our communication with God, however, it is the deeply personal, mysteriously interconnected relation of I-You that is activated. We cannot pursue that relation, because it is already within us; the only requirement for connection is the willingness to listen.

I'd found comfort in this, because I guess it made me feel like (a) I had a shot at the God thing, and (b) I didn't have to do, or grasp at, anything that felt unsettlingly like bullshit. I could just be open to the conversation as it unfolded. For me, it began with my first child's birth. I'd always been a fourteen-hour-a-day working reporter, the essence of a nonbeliever. But the moment the doctor placed this little boo-boo at my breast, and we gazed at each other, I was hit with The Big Love. When my second child was born, I was struck again. I knew right then that love *was* the secret of durable pigments, and because of it, none of us were alone. Not even the worm.

But I still wasn't sure that I was an okay mother. With Cal assuming so many of the traditional maternal functions, I was a little lost in my thoughts about what kind of mother I should be. It now occurred to me that my friend's sexist comment about staking out my own territory as the mother might be weirdly sensible. Still, I thought I brought a few things to the table. I knew, for example, that I definitely wanted to be a full-time stay-at-home working mom, and within that oeuvre, a *regular* mom. I wanted to have a home in which my children would feel cozy and protected, in which they could see all kinds of work being done: housework, professional work, hobby work. I wanted them to see that while each had its pleasures and irritants, work was an enriching, important, and inevitable feature of life. I wanted them to discover the kind of work that brought them pleasure, as well as to learn how to do the kind one simply must do but can learn to find pleasure in doing nonetheless.

In my particular idiom of maternal desire, I recognized something: I was more or less gravitating to the habitude of *my* upbringing. For all her eccentricities, my mom had demonstrated a pretty good work-life paradigm. I *did* want this gene encoded on my maternal DNA. But I didn't want to be the awkward, cerebral, workaholic mom, either. Because I wanted our family to be a part of the community, I wanted the other mothers not to regard me as a freak.

The other mothers. Much has been written and broadcast about the junior high school social phenomenon that takes immediate effect after one becomes a parent. Many a tech entrepreneur and award-winning documentary filmmaker has been brought to her knees on entering the mommy culture. Abandon here all the credentials you've spent years stockpiling on your résumé. You have to make all new friends, which often means entering the sticky social dynamic of a "new moms' group," a circle of strangers whom you may or may not end up even liking all that much but who share in the most intimate nuances of your early life as a mother. You're savagely vulnerable. Your hormones crash through you, one jolting tsunami after the next. You call each other a lot to compare notes. You see each other's transformed breasts a lot. You talk a lot about your new sexuality. You complain about your hormones. There is a lot of one-upmanship, conscious or not. There is a lot of time spent just hanging out with these people. In other words: junior high school.

Some of my closest prebaby friends prudently circumvented the intensity of the new mommy culture once they had children, either by working full time or just deciding to opt out. I couldn't do either. For one thing, Cal and I had reorganized everything so that we could stay at home with our children *and* work, so as viewed through the mommy culture lens, I was neither fish nor fowl. For another thing, we lived in Park Slope, headquarters of diverse, progressive family life in New York City. Long before we had even considered having children, I had lobbied Cal to move to Park Slope because I secretly felt that it was precisely the kind of neighborhood in which we could someday create such a life.

In 1994, Park Slope was still weird. It was a genuine mix of ages, races, and socioeconomic strata, a neighborhood of activists, writers, therapists, and people who joined the food co-op because they believed in communism, not just because they wanted cheap organic cereal. It was like Berkeley, only better because it was in New York. And I fit in. In fact, I didn't even seem like a freak except that maybe, because, like my mom, I loved clothes, I might have seemed a little fancy. Then again, I felt Cal and I both seemed a little fancy because we had a three-bedroom apartment with an eat-in kitchen—by far the nicest, most adult place the two of us had ever lived in New York and the perfect place to raise our child. But in the nearly seven years that had elapsed since Cal and I had moved to Park Slope, much had changed. I hadn't realized it until I joined one of the neighborhood mothers' groups, and I was utterly unprepared for what I encountered.

People our age with children *owned* their own homes.

FIVE

THIS MUST BE THE PLACE:
MAKING A HOME

In all the years that we had been together, it had never occurred to Cal or me to *buy* property. That was something that you did in the suburbs, or maybe in places like Washington, D.C., Houston, or Los Angeles. Not in New York City! That's what rent control was for. My aunt had lived on the Upper East Side her entire adult life without ever buying, and she was a fancy person. My godmother bought her longtime one-bedroom on East End Avenue only after the building went co-op, but she was a bona fide grown-up by that time. Another auntie owned her penthouse apartment on Riverside Drive because she was an heiress who had been married to an heir and had won the apartment in the divorce. Regular people, certainly people in their early thirties, didn't *own* New York City real estate.

Yet, yes, they obviously did, and they weren't crappy places in "transitional" neighborhoods. They were beautiful old co-op apartments and brownstones in *our* neighborhood. Not only that, but people our age were doing *home renovation*. They were hiring *architects* to redo their *kitchens*. They wanted the kitchens to be the heart and soul of their homes, the place where the family cooked together, ate together, nourished itself as a warm cocoon together. Where the hell had *I* been, all happy with my third-floor walk-up?

One low point with my mothers' group came when we all agreed to meet at one woman's house well past my bedtime so that all six of us could cook homemade baby food together in her eye-wateringly expensive kitchen. As I sat scraping fresh organic corn off the cob into a Le Creuset dutch oven perched like a smug grandmother atop the front burner on a six-thousand-dollar Viking range and oven, I felt like the new scholarship kid at an all-girls' private school, invited to a slumber party at the rich girl's house. *Shit*, I remember thinking. *How did I get back here?* I'd already been that kid. While I realized at that very moment that I was once again going to be the weirdo, I also knew two other things. First, my children were *not* going to be that kid. Second, I *definitely* wanted them to have their own soulful kitchen, too.

When I came home that night to our once-beloved rental apartment, I was twitching with shame and disgust. We were unbelievably shitty, irresponsible parents, I told Cal. We had bet the bank on stock options, minor players in the tech economy that we'd been. All that had gone up in flames. What were we doing to invest in our family's future? Were we really going to fritter it away by buying thousand-count pima cotton sheets and Gucci bucket hats? What were we *thinking*? We had been engaging in blind, desperate consumerism of the most pathetic order! Now, it seemed so obvious: By buying a home, we were investing in the health of our family as well as our financial future. He, stunned, agreed immediately. We should start looking tomorrow. But where would we get the money? How was everyone getting these mortgages—and how were they paying for these kitchens? Were we the only losers?

Much, much later—toward the end of 2008—I was reading about the mortgage credit crisis for the ka-trillionth time, thinking rancorously: Who *are* these people who got us in this freaking mess? Why didn't it occur to them that the banks were dangling fool's gold in front of them? You could maybe understand naïve, hopeful American dreamers getting sucked in, but what about all those educated white-collar assholes who took out jumbo mortgages with five-year ARMs and then HELOCed themselves to the hilt to finance remodeled kitchens with Sub-Zero refrigerators and soapstone countertops? What's *their* story?

Then, as I gazed wistfully around my crappy ghetto house, where I'd recently relocated with my children after my divorce compelled me to sell my beautiful, freshly gut-renovated brownstone in a nice neighborhood before the bank foreclosed on it—because there was no way, given my place in the national financial fiasco, that I was going to be able to afford the jumbo mortgage monthly payments alone—it came to me, as in the final scene of *Angel Heart:* I *am* those people. Many other Xers are those people, too.

It turns out that while we may have disparaged commercial culture as teenagers ("I don't buy anything that's *advertised*!"), we sure spend a ton of money as parents. We have created what is called the zero-to-three market, a $20-billion-a-year industry representing the first segment in "cradle-to-grave" marketing. My friends and I used to snort at yuppies for their cornball conspicuous consumption: the ludicrous flaunting of yachts, sports cars, caviar, cigars (I always think of that 1980s commercial for Gallo jug wine and its ascot-wearing spokesman smarmily asking "How do you think I got *so rich*?"). But according to market research, X spends more than yuppies ever did on luxury goods, especially if it has to do with home. Indeed, Gen X's rapacious need for the perfect nest drove them take out more home equity loans and spend more on house remodeling, per capita, than any generation before. In the mid-2000s, housing research analysts from Harvard's Joint Center for Housing Studies to the U.S. Census Bureau tracked our mass, and massive, investments in charming old houses in urban and outlying areas; banks now notoriously overextended to us subprime mortgage loans and home equity lines of credit so that we could remodel them into the homiest possible homes.

Marketers understand these spending patterns to reflect Generation X's desperate moves to invest in "home" and "happy childhood" before all else, even at the expense of retirement savings, health care, and political involvement. All this is, in traceable and ineffable ways, the fallout from the mass divorces and family breakdown of the 1980s. We may not be sensible to the precise qualities of these undercurrents, but we discern them in some murky, disquieting way. *The numbing, frigid desert of deep space:* We can feel it there, lying in wait just beyond our back doors, which are equipped with antiqued, nickel-plated Restoration Hardware knobs, latches, and hinges—amulets against the void.

You know the story. The scenario for today's prototypical middle-class Generation X homeowner follows the same drumbeat. We've already covered the rogue childhood, so let's just fast-forward to: you, having a solid career (which you did your *own* way, without toeing the line for anyone), getting married much later than your parents did (their *first* time, anyway), and having your first baby. Nothing in your life prepared you for how utterly white-light an experience holding that little biscuit would be. If nothing had ever been all that clear in your life, it was now: You'd do anything for this creature. By now, it was the late 1990s, early 2000s, and maybe you'd gotten at least a little whupped by the market crash in 2000, or more than a little by the downturn post-9/11. You were freaking: You needed stability, solid ground. You had *children.* Then interest rates dipped, enticing mortgages were unveiled, and the solution materialized like a fairy godmother: A *home!* Not the psychospiritual SRO of your childhood but a *homey* home. You'd invest yourself, your money, your family's financial future—your whole idea of familyness—in it. You jumped in, headfirst. You'd always been so self-reliant, so wary of easy schemes, that you didn't see at the time that you were getting in over your head.

Cal and I did, and we were, as it turns out, in generational company. In the fall of 2005, Generation X had higher home ownership rates than any previous generation, in spite of the recent housing bubble. In 1983, when older Baby Boomers were in their thirties, more than 60 percent of them owned their own homes; a decade later, that number dipped to 55.8 percent for younger Baby Boomers in their thirties. In 2005, more than 61 percent of thirtysomethings, now Generation X, owned homes. Why? A major reason, the report pointed out, is that Generation X was much more likely to look at their home as an investment than previous generations, owing largely—you guessed it—to having lived through the '90s recession, followed by the stock market losses in the early years of the twenty-first century.

For those of us crawling our way out of the wreckage of the dot-bomb period, that's what made those low or no down payment and ARM mortgages so irresistible. Indeed, surveys conducted by the National Association of Realtors show that four out of ten first-time buyers used no-money-down mortgages in 2005 and 2006; the median down payment for first-time buyers in those years was just 2 percent. What this seems to mean is that the collective feeling was, basically, screw stocks, invest in a home, and pay for it when you get back on your feet.

This evidently seemed like a no-brainer for phoenixlike Xers. We'd always landed on our feet. For one thing, we're not only better educated than Baby Boomers, but we made more money than they did, too, with median incomes nearly 50 percent higher than older Baby Boomers and $12,000 higher than their most immediate predecessors in the younger Baby Boom. So what if the housing prices were so high now that we couldn't afford to buy? "If we use education as a proxy for future and potential wealth," surmised the JCHS report, "this indicates that members of Generation X carry the same potential for high future earnings." Right! That's what we were thinking, too! Indeed, Xers in 2000 had higher levels of confidence in their own financial situation than any other generation—"an indication," concluded the Harvard report, "that Gen Xers have more actual or perceived opportunities for upward financial mobility."

Far be it from the banks to have disabused anyone of that notion. That was Cal, me, and, after months of home hunting, our bank. In fewer than six months after the late-night baby-food-a-thon of shame with the mothers' group, Cal and I became hard-core yuppie real estate porn addicts, compulsively hitting the refresh button on the *New York Times* real estate section online a jillion times a day, taking walks in our neighborhood not for the fun of it but to scout the FOR SALE signs of low-rent Brooklyn-based real estate firms that might offer better deals than white-glove Manhattan-based outfits. Everything was getting so damned *expensive*! We despaired. We should have bought something *years* ago! Maybe we just had to face it: We couldn't afford to live in the city anymore.

We took weekend trips to the New Jersey suburbs, where an exodus from Park Slope had been steadily headed for the past several years. We were driven around by pleasant real estate agents, sitting in the backs of their station wagons with Zanny patiently babbling in her car seat, watching the rows of 1920s Cape Cod, colonial, and ranch-style houses undulate by. We were led into many of these places, climbed their carpeted staircases, circled their kitchen islands, witnessed the sports trophies in the children's rooms. All I could envision was our children as teenagers in a suburban wasteland, driving around drunkenly to the next party where the parents weren't home: my own adolescence. For Cal, it was the ultimate knock to his first-generation immigrant ego: settling for second best because he couldn't hack it in the big leagues. I said: "I hate it, too, but this could be a great move for the children—do we really have a *good* reason for putting the kibosh on Jersey?" Cal accelerated toward the Goethals Bridge. "Yes," he said. "I don't want to."

But something else was afoot for Cal and me, too. I couldn't put my finger on it exactly; mostly, it seemed exciting and strangely grown up. Having our babies had not made me feel grown up in this kind of capacity. Having the babies brought about an intimate, profound transformation: I'd been instantly forged into a real *human* with a soul. But this home-buying gauntlet was a categorically different rite of passage. There were documents requiring signatures in a hundred different places, binding us to a hundred different legal stipulations; there were banks investigating our financial histories and making long-term projections about our future as employable taxpayers; lawyers, notaries, agents, secretaries were all summoned and working to vet and authorize the legitimacy of our role in the transaction. If having children had inducted us into the deeply sweet and complex realm of humanity, buying property was indoctrinating us into incontrovertible adulthood. We were grown-ups now: an actual married couple, doing what actual married couples did. It was kind of awesome. But there was also something disquieting about it.

As the momentum generated by our compulsive scouring of interest rates and mortgage packages grew more and more giddy and frenzied, something in our center of gravity began tilting. Certainly, we were both obsessed, discussing nothing but percentage points, paint colors. But Cal had never been so on fire about anything. He was hounding real estate agents, tracking down the perfect loan, calculating closing costs. And he was determined to find the kind of place he wanted. Each time we'd allowed ourselves to look at a property that he loved but was out of reach for us financially, he was genuinely defeated. I floated the idea of moving to another Brooklyn area, where prices were cheaper. "I don't want to live in some crappy place in a shit-bag neighborhood!" he'd rail. I knew how he felt, but what could we do? This was our first place, a starter home; it was *supposed* to be modest. We shouldn't feel bad about that. "I just can't do it," he said. "I want a *nice* place." He was anxious, sleepless. It ate at his ego. It would make him "feel like shit" to see those other "smug" parents in the neighborhood with their "sweet places" while we had "nothing." He knew he was being hyperbolic. But he couldn't help it. He couldn't rest.

The place Cal and I liked most *was* nice—it was perfect. It was out of our price range. He had taken his parents to see it. "It is beautiful—it has 'old world charm,' " said his mother. "But you cannot afford it." Cal was furious. He should have gone to medical school, at least law school, his mother snipped. *Oof.* But she had a point. We weren't doctors, lawyers, or bond traders; we were a writer and an independent consultant. Maybe we just had to come to terms with the blunt truth that we had been priced out of our neighborhood; a lot of other people in our position had moved into other spots in Brooklyn and were making it work. Plus, if this area was becoming so yuppie and rich, did we really want to be here, anyway? Fuck them! We should concentrate less on the real estate end of this and more on making a genuine *home.* Cal went into a funk. So he was just going to have to raise his kids in a *dump? That's* how it was going to go for him? He wasn't going to *get* the nice place—that's all there was to *that.* He watched TV late into the night, was detached and grumpy during the day. His swagger faded.

I couldn't figure it out. I wanted a nice place, a homey home, too—*definitely* wanted it. But the status element, while it had its devilish appeal, didn't seem like such a big deal. It was shattering for Cal. I'd never seen this in him. But when I thought about it more, I realized that perhaps it had always been there, just in a slightly different form. That Cal had always enjoyed incontestable authority among his friends, and certainly inspired a great deal of it in his business dealings, was a given. That I had always relied on his sense of confidence was also a given. But the more I contemplated his struggle with this whole real estate brouhaha, it began to dawn on me that perhaps his sense of authority and confidence was more tenuous than I had imagined. Perhaps, in some way, it hinged on the very appearance of authority and confidence. That is, he *needed* a nice place in order to uphold his sense of competence, and that without it as bolstering context, he would feel exposed to others, to himself. The system would disintegrate. I panicked. I might want a home, but *he needed that place.*

I convinced Cal to help me lobby each set of parents (except my father) to lend us some money to make a good-sized down payment, and with a five-year ARM, we would be able to afford the monthly payments. We threw caution to the wind, bid, and won the place we wanted: a gorgeous three-bedroom co-op in a prewar limestone building in the best school district in Brooklyn. I remember the loan officer at WAMU telling Cal and me that although we were cash poor now, he could tell we were the kind of people who would make money in the future. We were the kind of people, he said, that the bank wanted to "invest in."

We didn't question the banks' pretzel logic any more than we did our own, and neither, apparently, did the majority of Xers. We trusted ourselves, the banks trusted us, we trusted the banks. Again, so say the numbers. According to research, members of Generation X in 2000 had more faith in the financial industry than previous generations at the same age. Evidently, we were so collectively sure of our own against-all-odds capabilities that it didn't strike us as odd that the banks should be, too—even though we had provided them with no actual proof that they should.

And, as usual, in a Psychology 101 way, it makes some sense. One of the notorious legacies of Generation X's home-alone childhood is an abiding suspicion of authority. All this has been well documented, e.g., we hate ass-kissing the boss, so just let us do our thing because we rock as self-starters. But when the whole housing bubble started to swell, the dynamic shifted: Enter the banks, as approving parents. At last! They gave us a *home*! It was as though we were finally getting the apology and consolation prize we'd always secretly hoped for: You didn't get a real home as a kid, but you worked hard, succeeded on your own steam, and now we're going to give it to you and *your* children. Welcome home. You earned it.

In a few months, we moved into our new apartment: a little perfectly cut jewel. It was on the top floor of a lovely 1910 limestone building on quite possibly the prettiest block in Park Slope. It was small, but the layout was ideal for us to build a family in, and I was soon pregnant with our second baby. And it was a *homey* home; you could feel the historical happiness embedded in its details. The bedrooms were nests, barely big enough for the beds they contained, but that was fine, because they were soft and cozy, with no room for the kind of clutter that can distract one from the important conduct of quiet and slumber. Our lives were lived in the living spaces, which were large and lovely. The entrance hallway was ample and welcoming and led directly to a massive Edwardian dining room, complete with a nonfunctioning but pretty maroon-tile-lined gas fireplace. Lumbering old wooden pocket doors separated it from the also massive living room, complete with functioning wood-burning, wood-manteled fireplace. The ceilings were grand, punctuated at the center with period chandeliers and festively bordered with egg-and-dart crown molding. These rooms, though originally designed to be pretentious, were made warm with our kooky mishmash of stuff—all laden with familial meaning. I should say, laden for *me*.

By his own admission, Cal's decorating preferences had, when we were living separately, tended to the 1980s single-guy variety: black furniture and media consoles. The décor of his own childhood home was decidedly not to his taste: reproductions of French Impressionist paintings, fussy Victorian settees, the white baby grand. I felt strongly, perhaps hysterically, that our home should look and feel like *home*. Cal shrugged. I could steer the decorating; he didn't care. In my ideal, home should reflect our current and past family history. With that in mind, the dining room served as a mixed-use space: eating center and art studio for our children. Since meals with very young children meant getting food shrapnel all over the floor, I figured it was okay to get art-related shrapnel all over the place, too.

They had an easel with actual tempera paints, clay, and tons of crafts supplies. I framed their pictures and paintings and hung them on the most expansive wall in the dining room in a rotating exhibition. The apartment's long hallway was the perfect venue for curating family photographs.

Populating our home's remaining territory were things I had grown up with in my childhood home before it split apart. One of the things that had been so devastating following my parents' divorce was seeing all of our things in separate houses. Over the years, both parents had pruned back a good deal; a lot of the stuff that had been so important to me was no longer important to them. So whenever they were getting rid of things, I appeared in a car with an open trunk. Now, everything was here, it was all *together.* My children and I would share the same sort of attachment to these odd things, not valuable in the *Antiques Roadshow* sense, but so deeply imbued with importance and place that each was like a talisman.

Virtually everyone on my dad's side of the family was a painter, and we had nearly all their extant pictures on our walls, just as they had been in my childhood home in Berkeley. There were my grandmother Thomas's still lifes with fruits and flowers above the sideboard; there were my great-grandfather Harvey's landscapes encircling the dining room table. My aunt Hannah's pen-and-ink portrait of Virginia Woolf hung over the comfy leather armchair in the living room, and the chef d'oeuvre—my dad's oil painting of four abstract apples suspended against a mossy green backdrop—crowned the mantelpiece.

From my mother's side, there were other things: the silver-plated Victorian lamp from my nana's farm in Virginia; the cigar box that Batista had given my great-grandfather Dawson (who had been the first ambassador to the Organization of American States), as well as a pair of drawings of gauchos presented to him by the ambassador of Argentina; silk Japanese kimonos collected by my great-great-aunt Emma-Jane, who, as a young widow, had taken a trip to "the Orient" in 1909. In a world where clean lines and contemporary furnishings ruled, our home was higgledy-piggledy, but it made me feel unreasonably happy, peaceful. "Where did you *get* all this?" an amazed friend once asked. To which, of course, I could only respond in Carlinese: "This is my *stuff*, man." By which to say, it was home.

But after living there for a few months, I realized that one major thing that I did not know about a home was how to care for one. Indeed, thanks to my matrilineal pedigree of nondomesticity, I knew dead nothing about it. When I came into my own household, at thirty-four, I realized that this was a big deal. It was a little like discovering one day that you have an unseemly tic that you never knew you had—like nervously scratching your armpits when you don't know what to say or farting when you're asleep—but that everyone else thinks of as being one of your distinguishing attributes. You feel like (a) How could I have gone so far in life without knowing about this? (b) Why didn't anyone close to me tell me I had this, knowing that I'm the kind of person who would definitely want to know about it? and (c) What am I going to do about it now, as in right this second?

My first response was to buy Cheryl Mendelson's *Home Comforts: The Art and Science of Keeping House*. People talk about *War and Peace* being a tome. *Home Comforts* is a *tome*. Its nearly thousand pages on setting up and maintaining a clean, well-ordered home begin with one of the most perfect lines of postfeminist nonfiction writing I've ever read: "I am a working woman with a secret life: I keep house." Mendelson, a Ph.D. in philosophy and a lawyer, grew up under the tutelage of her two grandmothers—one Appalachian, the other Italian—who raised her to be a rural housewife, not only instructing her on every last aspect and aim of housekeeping, but also teaching her that the work itself was essential and gratifying. To be clear, it is not a memoir of "my life with two housekeeping grandmas" but a forthright and exhaustive guide to washing, laundering, mending, marketing, list making, cleaning, sewing, repairing, cooking, baking, food label reading, tending, dusting, sorting, tidying, ironing, folding, system making, everything.

I devoured this book. I devoured it as if it were every "just like Mom used to make!" cookie I'd ever seen advertised but on whose inspiration I'd never snacked. With its vivid, earnest descriptions of chores, it was a small, magical world, like *Little House on the Prairie*. Schedules for household tasks! One for each day of the week! Washing on Monday, marketing on Tuesday, minicleaning on Wednesday, odd jobs on Thursday, housecleaning on Saturday morning! Guidelines: Proceed from higher to lower; dry to wet; inside the house to outside; begin with the chores that require waiting times! To learn about those things that make a home ineffably homey—sweet, laundered sheets; ordered, airy rooms; clean bathtubs and fixtures; good meals; books, mended; socks, darned—was like randomly flipping to a psalm for the heck of it and unexpectedly actually finding comfort in it. Order in Homes—it *did* exist! My children would know it, even if I hadn't.

One of the other things I liked about Cheryl Mendelson was her husband. Edward Mendelson was a professor at my alma mater and academia's preeminent Auden scholar, not to mention the executor of Auden's estate. Ed was also a contributing editor at *PC Magazine* because he loved computers and writing about them. The idea that Auden, technology, Cheryl, and Ed were all somehow mixed up in a Laura Ingalls Wilder milieu of old-fashioned housekeeping appealed to me on every possible level.

Her invocations of Auden's *About the House*—a collection of poems that map the architecture of a home and its correlates in the mind, body, and spirit—were especially poignant. My sophomoric reading of *About the House* had been predicated on the idea that the whole thing was symbolic, home included. Indeed, even my understanding of the required undergraduate study of architecture in general—Gothic cathedrals, say, modeled on the body of Christ—had been grounded in my assumption that the purpose of *all* construction was symbolic. Jesus, I really *was* a WASP.

Reading this book, I realized that I honestly had had no real awareness that one could actually find a sense of soul, even transcendence, at home, in a church—in an indoor place. I was positively blown away when in her section on caring for the kitchen—a chapter rife with notes on glasses, flatware, utensils, bakeware, pots, pans, and the materials used in cookware and their properties—she invoked the Auden poem "Thanksgiving for a Habitat," which describes the kitchen as "the centre of a dwelling," a "numinous" place in which "ghosts would feel uneasy." That is precisely what I wanted to do in our home—no bad ghosts from childhoods past.

But to do it, Mendelson seemed to suggest, would require a certain degree of yielding, of relinquishing unhelpful ideas about division of labor, power, men and women. As in: It's okay to be a housewife. She mused on what some of the more rigid thinking attending the women's movement had done to bulldoze the home and the womanly art of caring for it, as well as media's role in underscoring "degraded images of household work and workers." Mendelson argued that what had been razed, along with all manner of yellow-wallpapered prisons, was love, comfort, and the sweet sense of belonging. "Unfortunately, what a traditional woman did that made her home warm and alive was not dusting and the laundry," she wrote. "Her real secret was that she identified herself with her home."

Holy shit. Could I be that mom, that woman, that wife—that *home* for my family? Suddenly, that idea was, for me, downright countercultural. I was in. Like all recent converts to orthodoxy, I went a little nuts. Part of going nuts was based on a frank acknowledgment that if I didn't go overboard on the discipline, I'd never get going on it at all. I figured that once the routine was set and became deeply ingrained, it would become a part of me and our home, the way the altar of the church is actually the heart of Jesus, in Catholic churches anyway. But part of it was also that I was just *psyched.* Ever since I was little, I've loved messing around with lotions and potions, so the fetishistic, chemical aspects of housecleaning fit perfectly with that penchant. I concocted counter cleaners from distilled white vinegar and lemon oil, wood floor cleaners from apple cider vinegar and lavender, toilet and tub cleaners from baking soda and peppermint, furniture polish from mineral and nut oils and sandalwood. I made hand and body soaps and laundry detergent. I saved worn-out boxer shorts and crummy T-shirts and ripped them into rags. I created systems for organizing clothes, books, toys. I even made some headway with mail. Mostly, I loved cleaning and scrubbing and washing. Eight months pregnant with our second child, I did not hesitate to get down on my hands and knees with a scrub brush. I loved our little home.

One night, Cal was observing my born-again housekeeping with detached amusement. What was I *doing*? I plopped my pregnant tenement of a self down on the sofa while he watched TV from the armchair nearby. And I thought: Look at *us,* Cal and me. We are sitting in *our* home. Here he is, feet up in a wife-beater undershirt. Here I am, with swelling breasts and massively pregnant, for the *second* time. It's August. I have just been on the *floor,* cleaning. It struck me that there could be something outrageously delicious about this whole turn of events. I knew it was odd, but after moving into our own home, something primal and sexist shifted in me. Could we be becoming *man and wife?*

But I also had another, dissonant feeling: I didn't know anything about the contents of Cal's interior. It hit me that since Zanny's birth, we had been in parallel mode, like toddlers on a marathon playdate. Each of us was engrossed in handling, inspecting, and shepherding the moment at hand and then scuttling on to the next, aware of the other's presence but not interacting. We had made no provision to appreciate the resonance created by this relentless pageant of activity. Aside from our cursory *Everything is different now* exchange, we hadn't talked. Period. We had planned, we had executed. We had not ruminated, we had not conjoined. It was surreal. I had been absorbed in a conjugal fantasy, a psychosexual renovation, and Cal was not actually involved in it. There was a good chance that he hadn't noticed anything except that I was inexplicably cleaning with vinegar. This is exactly what Cal had been worried about that day in the park, just before I got pregnant the first time. But that could be changed. It could be made into a real moment. Cal always saw the extraordinary.

So I spoke. I told him how much it meant to me to actually care for our home, and, a little shyly, that in so doing I really wanted to try to be an actual wife and mother. I wanted our kids to be nourished by good food that had been made not just for them but for the whole family. I didn't want there to be "the children's table," with the kids quarantined in their own feral territory. I wanted that home to be one where my children's friends wanted to come, where they themselves felt wanted. I wanted our family to be friends with neighborhood families who came to that home so that everyone's children would feel swaddled by their community. *I want for you to be able to be the guy and for me to be the woman. That kind of thing. If you want.* "Susie, I think if it makes you feel good about yourself, then go for it," he said. "You gots to do what you gots to do."

As he sat there in the living room watching *CSI* with his back to me in the comfy leather armchair, the anchor ran out of rope. "Well, what about cooking?" I ventured hesitantly. "Do you think I should do some cooking, too—so it's not all on you?" He scratched and yawned. "I don't," he said. "A lot of the thing with cooking is technique, and it's not worth the time it would take you to get the hang of it—stick with what you're good at. But do you have to use vinegar?"

I could have pushed it. I could have grabbed the fucking clicker out of his hand, tossed it on the floor, and kissed him. I could have forced the moment to its crisis. But I didn't. I nodded. I lay back. I watched television. On the screen, the *CSI* team had just uncovered the secret lair of a fetishist. It was furnished with a giant mobile, a stack of enormous diapers, and a crib made for an adult.

Not long after that, I went into labor during the Northeast Blackout of 2003. I moaned in the dark: the heat, impenetrable. Mama mammal instincts must have sensed danger because the labor stopped for twenty-four hours. But then it kicked in again, and after ten hours of wild banshee bellowing, I gave birth to our second daughter, Pru. My merry-eyed little Pru! When I'd first laid eyes on Zanny, I had known that she was the person I'd waited my whole life to meet. When the doctor laid my Pru at my breast, I knew that I'd *already* known her all my life—she was just here now. We nestled into each other on the hospital bed, and I felt strong and happy, even in my sleep. My new baby bunny.

As delighted as I was, I was also profoundly pooped, and I flinched every time movement forced me to summon a limb. I had delivered Pru with nary a drug, and I had gotten pretty ripped up during pushing. I just wanted to sleep. Cal wanted me to come home. Zanny, though she had come to the hospital to meet her new sister just hours after birth, missed me; plus, family wanted to come over and meet the baby. The hospital wouldn't discharge me for at least twenty-four hours, so he went to petition the nurses. They were firm: We need to keep an eye on the baby, they said, and the mother needs to rest. We should really wait the standard forty-eight hours. "That's ridiculous," Cal said. "She can rest at home."

Almost twenty-four hours to the minute, I went home. The next day, Cal said that family was coming over. I begged him to put it off for at least a few more days. "But I've already told them that I'm cooking!" he said. Pru and I lay in bed while Cal cooked for his family on our roof deck.

It was via Cal's reign over the kitchen that our life expanded into the kind of life that I had always hoped for. Laundry is laundry, and clean floors are expected, but food is food. Cal was an excellent cook. He loved to cook for big groups, had grown up cooking for a houseful of approving relatives, had cooked for his fraternity in college for the fun of it. People always loved his food, and he took genuine pleasure in their pleasure. Because cooking was his métier, and I was a chatty Cathy, our home became a magnet for get-togethers.

We shared meals with families: the children tumbling and bumping into one another like puppies, the adults having the kind of iterative conversations one has with young children, stopping every few moments to broker peace negotiations or address a sweet concern. Because he preferred to stay in the kitchen or working the grill—the kind of cook who wants meal-making to be a focused, solitary meditation, not a group activity—my job became that of the gabby, self-deprecating hostess, making guests feel welcome and not guilty for shooting the breeze and allowing a sumptuous meal simply to appear before them.

So, even as Cal's and my foundation began rotting, our exterior became ever more polished and put-together. The more he cooked, the more I talked, and the more I talked, the more I felt my sense of manic kinesis returning. Keep moving. Inertial force. Talk, talk, talk.

Cal also insisted on doing the cleanup, arguing that he was so devoted to his system in the kitchen that he'd freak if anyone else "monkeyed" with it. No problem, everyone said, giggling at the ridiculous luxury that his obsessive drive afforded them. Talk, talk, talk. One of the children's favorite playthings was a wooden kitchen—a stove, an oven, a sink, and a cupboard containing miniature pots, pans, and dishes. Whenever they played kitchen, whoever was the "cooker" played the role of Cal; everyone else just *talked*. Once, when we were all eating dinner on our roof deck, the preschool-aged son of one of our closest family friends asked his father, "What's your favorite restaurant in our neighborhood, Daddy?" (All the little kids in Park Slope are boulevardiers before they're out of diapers.) Our friend said: "*This* is my favorite restaurant, man—the food is amazing, you guys get to horse around with *your* friends, and I get to hang out with *my* friends." It was a compliment. I laughed, loudly. A restaurant—where you go to get away from home.

I became known as the luckiest mother in the neighborhood. My God, you guys don't just have mac-and-cheese and broccoli—you're eating lambburgers with artisanal feta and homemade roasted peppers! You have chopped cucumber, parsley, and Greek yogurt salad every night! *And* he works from home, so he can pick up the children from school! And he's so *calm*! He's the only father you can trust completely—he's an honorary *mother*! *We're* having a conversation about our useless husbands now, Susie, so please just shut up and get us some coffee. An English mom friend once pinned me with a very British look and snapped pointedly: "Look, darling, you've basically married the perfect man—you don't have to do *anything*." She was right. Couldn't I do *anything*? One morning, Cal was running late. I said, "Go ahead, take a shower—I'll make breakfast." Breakfast was whole-wheat toast with organic almond butter and honey. I heard the shower start. I heard the shower stop. I heard footsteps padding down the hallway. Cal appeared at the kitchen door, skin not yet damp, in a towel. "Don't forget," he said nervously, "to take the toast out when it's browned." With my back to the kids, I flipped him the finger. He chuckled. I smiled thinly.

The centre of a dwelling. All of a sudden, our kitchen felt too small. It was definitely too small. And ugly. The floor was covered in 1980s-era black tile that had acquired an oily patina that all my scouring could not slough off. The counters were of black plastic laminate, also oily. The table was from Ikea, as was the bookcase where we stored the pots and pans. The appliances were embarrassing. No serious cook could get anything done in here. Practically everyone else we knew had a serious kitchen, but few were the cook Cal was. It didn't seem fair. Even though we'd already sunk all our retirement savings into the down payment, we should really take out a home equity line of credit and renovate.

Tear out the old stuff, throw it away.

Many, many people were doing it—not just in our neighborhood, though I have no doubt that the numbers could successfully demonstrate that Park Slope circa 2005–2006 was ground zero for expensive kitchen renovations nationwide. It was true in general for people our age across the country. The Harvard home modeling report's analysis was that Generation X's unprecedented confidence in its own grit, coupled with its equally high trust of banks, would translate into "higher likelihood of investment and consumption," and further, that "members of Generation X may be more likely to use banks for refinancing activity, leveraging home equity, and generally sustaining high levels of consumption." They're so smart at Harvard. During the housing bubble, Generation X did indeed spend more on home remodeling than Baby Boomers spent when they were the same age. We started taking out HELOCs to pay for that remodeling, and the banks let us because the housing market was so screaming. In 2005, home equity had more than doubled in a decade. We banked on it; everybody who owned a house banked on it. Indeed, the Harvard study reported that home equity alone was homeowners' most important asset, that *two-thirds had more home equity than stock wealth.*

But one of the chief reasons that Generation Xers spent more than other homeowners on remodeling was that we bought charming fixer-uppers—those vitally important *homey* homes. According to the Joint Center 2005 research, 31 percent of Generation Xers lived in homes that were at least forty-five years old, compared with 22 percent of Baby Boomers when they were in their thirties. New housing developments? No, thanks—we already saw *Poltergeist, E.T.,* and *Suburbia.* Dude, we *lived* it.

And the fixer-upper nesting phenomenon wasn't just limited to the coasts, either. In the spring of 2007, *Professional Remodeler* featured the growth industry in Kirkwood, Missouri, a suburb of St. Louis. The town's leading construction firm, Riggs Construction, estimated that 80 percent of its business came from Generation X buying up the bigger, older homes in town. We also spent more because we wanted to be *involved* in the renovation, *invested*; unlike previous generations, who typically just deferred to the expertise of a contractor or decorator, Generation X wanted to *be* architect, decorator, HVAC engineer—or at least dabble in those roles. "Generation Xers want to have a remodeler help them buy rather than sell them," David Alpert, president of Continuum Marketing Group of Great Falls, Virginia, a firm that works with remodelers around the country, told *Professional Remodeler.* "They want to make a selection from a series of choices, but they want the remodeler to help them make the choice more intelligently."

Not only that, but according to professional home remodeling firm research, Xers depend more on the advice of their peers than earlier generations. Tell me about it. In our neighborhood, sitting down in a friend's kitchen for a cup of coffee while the kids had a playdate basically involved passing your orals in some kind of Restoration Hardware version of dialectical materialism. "How did you guys seal your poured concrete counters without getting that icky 'satin' look?" and "Is it dumb to go with Carrara marble because it's so porous, or do you think stains just make it more homey?" and "Now, did you have to go somewhere upstate to get your claw-foot reenameled?" Useful footnotes were "Those Franke faucets are crazy expensive, but don't ruin your whole kitchen just because you wanted to save three hundred bucks at the time"and "Go with the Bosch dishwasher, definitely—it's so much quieter." By the time you walked out, you'd have the names of at least two really good, somewhat reliable general contractors (the best anyone can hope for); the most amazing (but pricey) wood-stripping guy in town; the best outlet for Wolf and Viking ranges; and the truth about Sub-Zero refrigerators.

That was in 2006. We took out a HELOC and cashed the fifty-thousand-dollar check I'd received from the estate of a wealthy family friend. We hired an architect friend and embarked on the yuppie odyssey that our neighborhood friends had undertaken. Cal was over the moon. A thorough and compulsive researcher, he read every review and product comparison of stoves, refrigerators, venting hoods, sinks, faucets, kitchen cabinets, and storage systems that could be found. We spent so many hours at the Brooklyn fancy appliance emporium of choice that we became friends with our designated salesman, Ira. We tweaked and retweaked the designs that our architect produced. We selected tile, tin ceiling panels, lighting fixtures, and marble countertop slabs from literally hundreds of choices. Our kitchen was enameled in paint chips. It was exciting. I love pretty things, I loved our home. It was adrenalizing to imagine a beautiful, reconfigured kitchen that expanded into our living spaces so that it would physically occupy the center of the dwelling, not just symbolically. But it also felt disquieting and counterfeit. Was this becoming Cal's and my real estate crisis, part deux?

I pretended that I just wanted to have a literate conversation with him about the principle of the thing, an aerial-view discussion. After all, I was in the middle of writing my book and was spending a great deal of my conscious time thinking about what compelled X parents to spend egregious sums of money on stuff for their children. You'd have to have been dead not to appreciate that there was something preternaturally bourgeois afoot in the zeitgeist. It was one thing to sit in the margins watching everyone else write their chapter of the home makeover narrative, lingering over the nuances of grout colors and bullnose tile. But it was another thing to be writing our own entry in this sociomaterialist history, and now that we were doing it, there was something unsettling about this undertaking. How could everything be so *expensive*? Didn't it seem bizarre that we were actually sitting here discussing the finer points of the fifteen-hundred-dollar refrigerator versus the five-thousand-dollar refrigerator? Didn't people just used to go to Sears when they needed a new fridge? Were we just doing this because everyone else was—were we Generation Jones people?

But even as all this came tripping off my tongue, I already knew what he was going to say. And that he would be furious. Cal was now the neighborhood cook; people depended on him to be that. He needed *nice* equipment. Why shouldn't he have it? The difference, Cal argued, was that, unlike many people, he would really *use* this equipment. Our restaurant-quality stove would not be used to heat sauces from jars; it would be used to *cook*. Furthermore, the kitchen was getting too crowded. He couldn't concentrate on making meals for all these people when they were up in his face constantly. *I* was the one who wanted to have people over all the time. If we wanted to do that, we had to have a place for them to sit! Plus, the girls deserved it. This was *their* home. Why wouldn't I want them to have a nice home, like all their friends?

Now I felt Cal's axis wobbling in a dangerously elliptical formation. I had a bad feeling. It occurred to me that maybe his center of gravity had depended on my not having one. Perhaps it was not coincidental that my efforts to generate one, or to merge my incipient one with his, had caused his to shift. Was Cal's center of gravity, of dwelling, shifting to the *nice* place, and this new kitchen? And in an odd, Greek-addled way, was this Cal's own reprise on the Carlin Room? Could it be that in the final analysis, he just wanted people to keep their grubby mitts off of his literal and metaphysical *stuff*? Did he just want to be *alone*? I couldn't even consider it.

So we went ahead with it. While the contractors bashed down our old kitchen and replaced it with a numinous one, we spent the summer living at my parents-in-law's house on Staten Island, and by the time the renovation was complete, we had spent more than a hundred thousand dollars. And the kitchen really *was* beautiful. It was right about this time that Pru, now three, developed not an imaginary friend but a place. She called it "my magical world." Her magical world included a house that was made entirely from roses. Its bedrooms were swathed in fairy bowers; the kitchen issued ice creams. She could describe this world in luscious detail, every time elaborating in a slightly different way. At the end of her exposition, she would always end with the sweet question: "Would you like to go to my magical world?" *Yes,* we would answer. *Yes, we would.*

One night, thinking about Pru's magical world, I read Auden's "The Common Life." I absorbed the lines about how in making a home, we build a fortress of privacy and protection from "the Dark

Lord and his hungry / amimivorous chimaeras." But in the end, the poem warned, our attempts are futile. Auden invoked a quotation from James Joyce: *The ogre will come in any case.*

Two years after the renovation was complete, we were driving on the Brooklyn–Queens Expressway. It was early summer, and the weather was perfect, like a sunny day in Los Angeles (extra perfect because it wasn't Los Angeles but New York). Cal, whose customary response to temperatures above 75 degrees was to seal the car hermetically and blast the air-conditioning, was inexplicably agreeable. Without an argument, or even a comment, he had allowed me to leave the windows down. The breeze was warm and riotous; the girls were giggling at the festivity of having it flip and whip their hair up and around. We were on our way to my in-laws' vacation house, a new construction in a complex by a golf course in the mountains of northern New Jersey. Years ago, I would have dreaded this whole scenario. Since then, Cal's mother and I had gone through tough periods twice—first when Cal and I were a new couple, then after Zanny's birth—but we had stayed the course and were now as close as I had ever been to any parental figure. I felt a sense of deep contentment because of that.

I remember that moment perfectly, as we headed toward the Verrazano Bridge. I remember thinking: Soak all of this in now, every little bit. Really listen to the giddy joy erupting in the backseat. Really appreciate your husband's small kindnesses. Relish the feeling of looking forward to spending time with your in-laws. Feel these things. Love *is* real. *Everything is different now.*

SIX

COUNTDOWN TO ARMAGEDDON:
MARITAL BREAKDOWN

When you talk to recovering alcoholics or drug addicts about their stories, one of the most striking themes is that no matter how bad it got, it never seemed to dawn on them that their problem was drinking or drugs until they hit bottom. "Denial" is the usual invocation, but that doesn't seem to cover this particular neurochemical trick. To deny something seems to me to require that one recognize the problem and then decide, consciously, either that it's not a big deal or that it isn't a problem at all. In these cases, the problem was never even identified. A young woman I know reports having peed into empty beer bottles when she was drinking alone in college so that she wouldn't have to use the common bathroom, lest she encounter a dormmate who might be "judgmental and weird." One man I met once used to turn tricks in the woods behind a rural turnpike truck stop so that he could buy crystal meth and bourbon. "I thought my problem was that I lived in a small, backward town," he said.

So it is, I have learned, for many of us whose marriages are disintegrating. Things get worse and worse, but there is not so much active denial as misattribution: "I just need time for myself," "He just hates his job," "We're so *tired* all the time," "It'll change when the kids get older." Certainly, these are all very real problems common to people with young children, and all have a corrosive effect on couples. But like the alcoholic narrative arc, things can get overwhelmingly bleak, and even worse, before the real problem reveals itself to you.

I now wonder if some of this blind spot isn't generational. After all, we married our soulmates; we are deeply attached to our children. Critical and contemptuous of how our own parents handled divorce and children, we think we know better and *have* done better. Whereas Baby Boomers outsourced the concerns of domestic life, Generation X husbands and wives share them: We are people, individuals—not roles, thank you very much. Few of us will admit, or commit, to abiding by any one polemic or philosophy: We take what we like, make it our own, and leave the rest. Whereas our parents regarded each other darkly through gendered lenses, Gen Xers view each other as friends, partners, compadres. X is famously proud of its approach: terminally unique. And it may be that such hubris is what makes us so blind to signs that our married lives may be falling apart. At least it was for me.

Like any two people who have been attached to each other for a long time, Cal and I had perennial quagmires. Affectations that had seemed charming at the outset had calcified into causes for grumpiness. I continued to reel from his TV watching, though I became inured to it. He thought my literary taste was rarefied and impenetrable, while I was disdainful of his fondness of the wizard-fantasy and space-opera genres. To Cal, this further confirmed what he thought already: I was a snob. Plus, he thought I was a blabber-mouth. He was (and still is) right. I walk into stores and chitchat with the proprietor; I always stop to talk to people I run into. It's one of the reasons why I liked being a reporter. I was aware that this was a point of difference from Cal, who was more aloof; that via my lo-gorrhea, he would become roped into frivolous conversations that he undoubtedly would have crossed the street to avoid. But I had al-ways thought that his irritation with my chattiness was, so far as character infractions go, on the same continuum as my irritation with his TV watching.

Same thing with his neatness and my sloppiness. Whether it is congenital or the legacy of an unkempt upbringing, I am a native slob. I am the kind of person who can leave dirty dishes in the sink overnight and not give it a second thought. Do them in the morning. Do them when you get home from work! I can appreciate that my sensibility is rather gross and guyish, but truly, I don't care. He did. He *super* did. The idea that food particles could be left to the open air for any longer than the time it took to eat them was so totally noxious to him that it pointed to the presence of some character de-fect lurking in the psyche of the person who could countenance such deviance. Early in our relationship, this contrast made for moder-ately funny back-and-forths about the Odd Couple, Lockhorns-era badgering, gender reversal, and so on. But this division—along with work issues and chattiness versus diffidence—became one of the most contentious and stressful issues of our sixteen-year relation-ship. Even after I had changed my habits, the ghosts of those defects continued to haunt us.

Maybe it *was* naïve and foolish to think, as I had, that marriage can change a person. But I do believe that its impact can at least pro-pel a person toward change; it had done so for me. I still, naturally, harbored feelings of incompetence and fraudulence, but overall, I had become a much happier person, had become interested in other people's troubles more than my own. I definitely wanted to be a better spouse and helpmate. Any residual problems we had, I was sure, were my fault.

In truth, they probably were. One of the mind-blowing things about being involved with a recovering narcissist is that the minute she stops behaving poorly, she wants everyone around her to share in her sense of accomplishment and closure. Ding-dong, everybody, the witch is dead! You can come out! We can be happy now! And of course, everybody is thinking: *Fuck you. We spent years as your hostages; now we're supposed to thank you for releasing us?* Cal claimed he did not feel that way. But swells of repressed anger and resentment do not evaporate; they just find another course. As Dr. Ian Malcolm said in such a Jeff Goldblumy way in *Jurassic Park,* "Life finds a way."

So. There were fights, fights that began as small, well-meaning criticisms of my maternal and domestic style and blossomed into larger, more all-encompassing ones. And they were not the angry, hand-gesturing psychic tussles of my youth, family of origin, and, in general, temperamental style. They were crackling, solitary wars played out in barbed digs, icy deadlocks, and silence. These wars were played out on Cal's turf.

One of the things we fought about was work. As established, I had vacuumed up the subject of work during our twenties. Then it was his turn: He launched his start-up company, and I supported him. Maybe it wasn't enough, and maybe it was too late. But one of the things that you hope for is that after you defer to your partner for a time—perhaps even a long time—things will even out, that a renewed, secure relationship will form. Four years into it, this still had not happened for us. He was furious, particularly about work. To be clear, he never said "I am still furious about work." He didn't have to.

We had one computer at home. We were supposed to take turns using it for work: he for his consulting company, me for my book. That his company had managed to remain standing in the carnage of the dot-com bloodshed was nothing short of miraculous, which said a great deal about Cal's preternaturally effective salesmanship. But it had been necessarily amputated to within an inch of its life to keep it alive, and supporting a family of four on its strength alone in New York City—never mind in wildly expensive Park Slope—was growing increasingly impossible. So getting the book deal had been not just a great thing for me professionally (especially since I had just about dropped out for two years) but also a genuine coup for our family. When we got the news, Cal and I had literally done the Hustle in the living room with our two-year-old and eight-week-old daughters, Zanny bopping around, dazzled by our boisterousness, and Pru, our little froglike newborn, open-eyed and astonished. We were going to make it—again! The money supplied by the book advance essentially doubled our combined income, which meant that though our work-family life would have to become the best-oiled machine in town, we did not have to live in constant fear. And we could buy books for the kids! And pay for private preschool! And go on family vacations!

But the thing about writing a book, as anyone who has written one or who has lived with someone who has written one knows, is that (a) you need big swaths of time to get any momentum going, (b) you need relative quiet during these times, (c) you need to hit your deadlines to keep your editor's, and your own, confidence afloat, and also to get paid the next installment of your advance, and (d) you actually have to write it. If these conditions aren't met, the chances that your book will not materialize are great. It's just the way it is, which is one of the reasons why books are hard to write (and you can multiply that by fifty if you are the mother of young children). However, the conditions for writing a book are not appreciably different for getting any kind of desk work accomplished. That was the case for Cal's variety, and we knew it would be difficult, particularly with no outside babysitting help.

Instead, we had our own child-care relay-race method. Was it a little insane for us? Yes! I was on a book deadline, still nursing Pru, and Zanny was in preschool only a handful of hours. But I would not have been able to work had I been worrying about what might be happening with my seriously little children with a sitter I didn't know well enough. I just would have lost my mind, period. I knew that this was an incredibly privileged position to be able to maintain. I also knew that my decision to make my life just this side of unmanageable stemmed from my own childhood experience of babysitters. Did my excruciatingly acute self-awareness give me pause? Certainly it did. Did it stop me? No, it did not. Our working friends thought we were nuts, but they empathized. In fact, fellow working mothers rarely, if ever, criticized our decision. No matter what any of us did, we all seemed to sense that there were actual trade-offs, something important that we would miss. There was no ultimate answer, no real rest. In this respect, it was like everything else that had always been on the insecure X continuum—job, field, location, family, even marriage. Maybe that's why we wanted the answer so desperately. Maybe that's why everyone thought Cal and I had it down.

And to the extent that anyone can have such a life down, we did have it down. While Cal worked in the morning, I would nurse the baby, take Zanny to preschool in the morning, nurse, play with the little one during the two and a half hours while our big one was at preschool, nurse, pick up the big one, give her lunch, nurse, bring everyone back in the early afternoon, and then pump breast milk, at which point Cal would take over so that I could work from midafternoon until evening. We always had dinner together. Bath time was also family time. Cal would bathe the little one and I would bathe the older one, each of us enjoying one-on-one time with the babies. I would then lie down with them, read stories, snuggle, and wait until they fell asleep, with the intention of sneaking out to debrief with Cal about our days. More often than not, however, I just fell asleep.

And more often than not, as time went on, the schedule did not work as planned. By the time it was my turn to use the computer, Cal would already be so engrossed in work that he could not stop, or would have been pinged by a client who needed to have a conference call right away, or his business partner would need him to cover, or I would conk out with the kids on returning home from preschool and forfeit my turn, or someone would get sick, or something else. It became clear after a few months of this that I was never going to be able to use the computer. My requests to use it enraged him. Fine, I could use it—he just wouldn't get his work done! Fine—he'd just have to tell that prospective client to forget it, that his company was just too busy to take on a new project. Fine—just tell him how we were going to pay the bills. The force of his outrage made me think that I was wrong to have asked, that he was supporting the family, of course. I didn't argue: I was wrong. Ultimately, I joined a writers' space in our neighborhood, ceding the home office to Cal. *God, you're so lucky,* friends in the neighborhood said. *I wish my husband was like that—what doesn't he do?* I had no answer—there was nothing. He did everything. Perfectly.

For Cal, control was paramount. It is true that living with someone whose inner weathers are tempestuous can drive even the most laid-back of souls to develop tics. But to those for whom a sense of control is inherently critical, it is disastrous. So even after I had made efforts to defer to his work schedule and to become a decent housekeeper, we both continued to operate as though nothing had changed—or rather, as if things had gotten *worse*. We went from the historical premise that I was a slob to the sense, somehow, that I was too inept to handle virtually any domestic task. We both believed it. This, like most developments of this sort, happened gradually; nothing was ever said explicitly. Soft pokes, over time, became sharp jabs. No offense, but my homemade cleaning products really *reeked*. And, actually, were they effective? Just wondering. I mean, it just didn't seem like things were really *clean*. Oh, I'd already scrubbed the bathtub? Oops, sorry about that—he couldn't tell. As soon as we got some more money, wouldn't it be great to hire a housekeeper? It would make *such* a difference to get the place really clean for once. Oh, no—*please* don't touch that pan! He had spent so much money on it, and it had to be washed in a special way, and he'd prefer to do it himself; he didn't want it to get ruined. Oh, God—don't clean the stove! Sorry, it was just a *really* sensitive piece of equipment. Don't put that knife in that slot—it doesn't go there! Just let him do it, *please.* Actually, if I needed something cut or chopped, could I just let *him* do it? Okay? *Please.* No, no, he'd make breakfast; the kids wanted pancakes, and they were used to *his* pancakes. No, no, he'd make lunch; he knew what the kids liked, and he had already planned it anyway. No—what would I make for dinner that the kids would *eat*? No, there was no point in my doing the shopping—how would I know what to *buy*?

And we went from the working premise that my propensity to being a chatterbox was an irritant to the two of us barely talking at all. This, too, happened over time. No, *you* set up the playdates—you're better at chatting with people than I am. No, *you* go to the teacher conference—you're so chatty, people respond to that kind of thing. Can't you ever just *walk down the street* without chatting? Do you always have to talk to *everyone*? Uh-oh, look out—Mama's going to start *chatting* now! (*No chatting, Mama! No chatting, Mama!*) Why should we hire a babysitter so we can go out to dinner—so we can spend a shitload of money just to *chat*? Why should we spend money on a babysitter so that we can go to a movie—can't we just wait for it to come out on DVD? Plus, if we don't have a babysitter so we can work, why should we have one just to go out? What are we going to do out that we couldn't do at home? Can you just let me watch TV? There's nothing to talk about.

By the time our older daughter was six, we had been out, as a couple, no more than ten times. He didn't want to. It wasn't just me. Cal's friends still invited him out to concerts and parties every so often, but he never wanted to go. He didn't want to stay out that late, he said; he'd be a wreck for the kids the next day. Then go out for just a little while, I would urge; no one is asking you to go out until two in the morning. They have nannies, au pairs, rich parents, he'd say; their lives are different, not hard like ours. I countered: But I'll stay at home—you go out! It's not hard! And also, our life did not *have* to be hard; we were, at some level, choosing to make it hard. Since we didn't have a sitter during the workweek, I argued, it actually made a lot of sense to ask someone we knew well—or at least his parents, who lived only fifteen minutes away!—to take care of the children for a few hours just once a month so that we could have a date. Even people who had full-time child care did it; they even went out together once a week. It would be a healthy thing to do, important for us as a couple. We needed a break! He didn't want to. It was too disruptive to the family schedule, to his rhythm.

He didn't want to. My initial thought was that he had fallen into a serious rut—maybe even a mild depression—and needed help shaking out of it. Beyond the communications breakdown, the classic signs were there. He didn't leave the apartment if he could avoid it. He'd always been a solid dresser; now, he wore the same outfit virtually every day, changing only his undershirt. His threadbare jeans and flapping sandals, and his unaccountable refusal to buy new ones, became a running joke with the few family friends we now saw. Cal and I laughed about it in their presence, but after they left, I would raise the issue more earnestly. Hanging on to those things has become ludicrously symbolic, I'd say. You're hanging on to a system that no longer functions, and it's literally undermining you. Bartleby the Scrivener, man! The weird guy in *Office Space*! Come *on*! He was not amused. He didn't want to change, didn't want help, didn't want to talk about it.

Maybe he and his business partner should rent a cheap workspace, just to get out of the house? I found him a rent-controlled one-bedroom in the city, near our subway line, that was laughably inexpensive. He didn't want to. That was an *outrageous* suggestion, he spat. Not only would it be a waste of *money*; it would be a waste of time *commuting*. Who would make *dinner*? So maybe the real problem was that he wasn't happy with his job; he should think about what he would really like to do. He was a phenomenal chef—maybe he should look into the restaurant business, or at least cooking school? He didn't want to. That was just *crazy,* he said. When would he have the time for *that*? Maybe he was unhappy, depressed—maybe he should see someone. Are you *kidding*? He didn't want to.

And then there was the matter of sex.

Since the first woman gave birth to the first child on earth, the sex lives of the parents of young children have taken a nosedive. But Generation X parents, it seems, are diving headlong into the abyss. In 2008, *The Journal of Sex Research* published the results of a study on "sensual and sexual marital contentment in parents of small children." Six years prior to the report, researchers had tracked the sex lives of 452 parents whose babies were six months old; they were reevaluated four years later. "Sexual contentment remained low," the study said. "More parents had changed from being sensually content in 2002 to discontent in 2006, than the contrary." Even those who hadn't had a second child weren't back to their pre-parenthood sex lives: "The average sexual frequency was low both at six months and at four years for both parents with and without additional children." Moreover, a 2005 study of more than eight hundred parents had discovered that "the majority of parents had sexual intercourse once to twice a month when the baby was six months old."

Sex, sex, sex. One of the focal points of my ambling thoughts and conversations about marriage in the last year of my own was sex. Not an original theme, but what began to become profoundly clear was that people who had formed a strong sexual union before having children were stronger in their marriages than those of us who hadn't. Again, perhaps not surprising, but it came as kind of a clarion revelation. This came into stark relief a few years later when I found myself engaged in a surprising conversation with an Orthodox Jewish acquaintance who was describing nuptial guidelines in the Orthodox tradition. Isaac said that when he got engaged, he had to enroll in the requisite marriage preparation class for men, which is taught by the synagogue's rabbi. Such classes are essential, since, if you've been a "good Jewish boy," he said, you have never even grazed a woman other than your mother or sister. Since these young men know nothing, practically speaking, about sex, a vital function of the classes is to teach them how to be good husbands in that department. Isaac said that everyone, obviously, feels ridiculous and embarrassed to have to learn the finer points of pleasing your wife from your religious counselor, but, he said, the rabbi emphasized the importance of knowing what you're doing. In Orthodox Jewish law, a rabbi must issue what's called a *get* to make divorce official. The rabbi told them that the underlying cause of 99 percent of the *gittin* he had personally overseen was an unsatisfactory sex life.

Ninety-nine percent. Instinct dictates that Isaac's rabbi may have inflated that statistic a shade for emphasis. Still, his message is one that any couples therapist would, and does, underscore, and it supports a theory of my own about why sex is so important in a couple's life now, post-children. In the first three years of a child's life, virtually every part of a couple's previous relationship and dynamic is stripped bare. The child's needs are so urgent, and so constant, that one is almost always in a state of triage, even when happy. There is no possibility of nuanced pillow talk; your brain is just fried. Furthermore, our generation does share child rearing (at least much more than any other), and by the time we have children, both members of the couple have built at least some part of their identity on work. This means that we don't have much appreciation for each other's differences and separateness during those early years in our children's life—and that, I believe, can lead to malaise, resentment, and hostility.

If you, for example, are taking care of the baby and your husband is going off to work, you have a pretty good idea of what his day is like, having gone off to work yourself for a good deal of your life. You are then in a position to compare your day with his, and you decide that you are resentful because his day does not compel him to be so relentlessly alert and responsive. When your husband watches you feed the fussy baby with some difficulty, he may feel free to criticize your style, having perfected a style of his own that seems to work beautifully. Because everyone knows everyone's business, there is no respect for each other's expertise; neither can claim it, because both have it.

Except in the area of sex. This is the one relation at this stage of life in which appreciation of differences and separateness are essential, capable of dissolving resentment and enmeshment. Good sex yields a sense of having been imprinted by the other, even as it lends a sense of mystery. If you don't have this sense of sexual union, or haven't had it at one point in your relationship, you end up with what's left: malaise, resentment, and hostility. This is not to say that you don't love your child with every vein, bone, and sinew in your body. But unless you have that strong sexual bond, it seems safe to say that having a baby won't bring you closer together. It will drive you apart.

In light of this theory, that outcome was perhaps even more inevitable for us. For one thing, since we both worked from home, there was zero mystery about what the other was doing with his or her day. We saw it all. No wonder Cal said there was nothing to talk about at the end of the day. For another, it wasn't that the traditional gender roles were askew, or even neatly reversed, in our relationship. We both behaved as though he was doing everything, and that he should, because I was incompetent to do it. We both believed it. It was not unlike a yuppie, Gen-X egalitarian take on *The Yellow Wallpaper* in which we were both, in our own ways, prisoners of that stifling attic room, isolated and unable to appreciate the pathology of our rapport. To us, and to everyone else, it seemed we had solved the thorny riddle of having it all. But the moment the door first creaked open and an outsider got a peek in, it felt as though a routine police check had stumbled upon bound hostages in a bunker.

I had been helping out an old friend—a single mother—by picking up her daughter from day care a couple of times a week and taking her, along with my daughters, back to their apartment (the girl felt more secure at her own home), feeding everyone dinner, and playing with all the little monkeys until my friend came home from work. It was fun. One evening, I guess I seemed blue, and my friend asked me what was up. Oh, you know, Cal's stressed and mad, but who can blame him, I said. You know what an incompetent I am. There was a pause. No, I don't, said my friend. Well, you know, I said, I can't even make dinner. My friend put both hands on the table and looked me in the eye. You got a major book deal, are writing the book, and are making your deadlines, without child care; you pick up your own children, and my child, from school; you make everyone dinner; you talk to me about my problems when I get home from work; you are funny and lovable. When I tell my colleagues about everything you do, they laugh. You, she said, are a parody of competence. *Anyone can make dinner.* I stared. Then, I sobbed.

What should Cal and I have done differently? Some would review our decisions and say that in the final analysis, it was the family bed that did us in. Ideally, you're supposed to sneak out of the family bed to have sex in another room. As the children get older, you're supposed to work on phasing them out by having them sleep in little nests on the floor beside your bed or moving them into their own shared room (which we had done, with varying degrees of success, depending on the night). It is not supposed to drive a wedge into the fissures in your relationship with your mate. The family bed is not supposed to become an excuse to avoid each other. But polemics are handily plastic, often allowing people to use them as a screen to avoid confronting some other, murky matter of personal discontentment.

It was no fault of the children's, of our decision to do it, of the practice itself. I wouldn't have done it any differently. I loved cuddling with my babies at least as much as, if not more than, they did. I don't know whether any of their sense of confidence and security can be traced to the family bed, but it certainly didn't hurt, and I don't think either Cal or I minded hedging our bets in any case. The point here is that if Cal and I had had a different dynamic—which is to say, an immutable sexual bond—the family bed might have come to symbolize not a gulf but a bridge in our relationship.

Friends tell me that it did in theirs. Some women have told me, for example, that prior to having children, their mates had seen them as sexual, but still in a teenage boy kind of way. But after having children, seeing their wives nursing, having the babies in the bed, their mates' whole idea of womanhood was expanded. For that matter, some women report that their husbands viewed pregnancy as the ultimate expression of their sexual connection. One woman said that her husband confessed after the fact that he had had an erection during her labor. While she was glad, certainly, that he had waited to tell her this until her stitches had healed, she also thought it was kind of awesome. I confess to being rather blown away by this, but okay. For me, the takeaway here is that sexual relationships are powerful by anyone's reckoning, and particularly so between a couple with children.

Cal and I had not slept alone in the same bed since we had had our babies. In the final four years of our marriage, we had not slept in the same bed at all. I was always in the kids' room, in bed with them; Cal slept alone, in ours. There had never been reason to do anything else.

At some point, the meaning of my stepsister's wedding present, our combined astrological chart, dawned on me: Being parents was the big cosmic purpose of our relationship. Before we had children, Cal had, consciously or not, operated as my parent. But Cal was an *actual* parent now. I had no pull; I had been severed. He was orbiting in an entirely different system now. *He didn't want to.* He didn't want to be with *me*.

Six months before my book was due to my editor, I got a call from my aunt. How long had it been since I had spoken to my dad? she wanted to know. I don't know, I said. A while. The truth was that it had been quite a while, maybe more than a year. We had not really had much contact since September 11, 2001. I suppose that means you don't know, my aunt said. Know what? Your father has bone cancer, she said. He has six to nine months to live.

My aunt's phone call came in February 2005. Dad didn't want us to come until summer. So we went that summer. They did not want us to stay in their house; we rented a neighbor's vacant house down the street from them. Zanny, then four, trotted around, trying to talk to my dad; he barely at looked her. He was preoccupied with erecting a giant mosquito-killing contraption that looked like a 1970s movie robot. After a day of this, Cal and I took the children to a nearby farm to feed baby goats and sheep. *What did you expect?* Cal said. The next morning, we found a note on our windshield: "Thanks for coming. Love, Dad." He was gone, had left for work at five-thirty that morning, his wife said, though we all knew he wasn't working anymore. "Your father is not good at good-byes," she explained, in a tone that seemed calculated to beam mysterious wisdom. I felt an angry dissertation welling up in me, but I smiled thinly instead and turned to strap the babies into the car. *Thanks for the visit,* Cal said.

The day after Halloween 2005, I called my dad. Pru had decided to go as both Frog and Toad, the eponymous characters of the children's books. All night long, she had had an expression on her face that was pure Dad: his signature "give me a break" look. It was uncanny; Cal had remarked on it, too. Dad would like that.

As I dialed his number, I was walking toward the Brooklyn Writers' Space, down Third Street in Park Slope. The sidewalk was mortared with candy wrappers, leaves, and indecipherable remnants of costumes. It was chilly and clear, and though it was morning, the fall sun was already on its trajectory to set.

At first I thought I was going to get an answering machine. But after a number of rings, my father's wife answered breathlessly, and on hearing my voice, she passed me to someone else. It was a hospice worker. "If you want to see your father alive, you should come within the next twelve hours," she said. Ian, coincidentally, had called their house about an hour before. No one had planned on calling either of us.

By the time I got there early that evening, my father was in a coma. He was laid out in a cot in his bedroom, mouth open. His glasses were off. He was howling. The house seemed to be shaking with it.

His wife, sitting Indian-style in an armchair, said that she thought he wanted to be alone, that if he were an Inuit, he would have walked out into the snow by himself. I looked at her. I was not going to let my father, *my dad,* die *alone.*

For ten hours, I crouched at his side. I held his hand. I put my head on his chest. He wailed like Lear on the heath. It was a horror. I whispered, for ten hours: "You are not alone. I am here. It's okay." My Daddy-Doe. My noodler-in-chief.

When the sun came up, the breathing had become less regular, and the howl had quieted. My brother, who had been sleeping on the bed, woke up. My father's wife materialized at the doorway. She sat on the bed and, petting their dog ceremoniously, informed us that she had consulted a medium a few months before, and that the medium had confirmed that she and Dad had not only shared their past lives together but would continue to do so throughout eternity. Ian and I looked at each other. After a long moment, I reminded Ian of a time we were all at the movies before our parents had split, when Dad had been in a really, really bad mood and had given my brother the popcorn to hold. My poor brother had been so nervous about the bad mood that he spazzed out with the popcorn, jerking a quarter of it all over the floor. Dad shot him an angry look, and he sprayed it out all over again. Every time he did it, Dad would bark, "Jesus, Ian!" and all my brother could say was, "Jeez, sorry, Dad!" But he couldn't stop; he was the oscillating popcorn sprinkler. Dad finally started cracking up, and the three of us had stood in hysterics in the lobby of the theater, with everyone staring at us, half-smiling in uncertainty about what sort of moment this was.

Ian and I sat on the bed giggling. Suddenly, Dad grunted. At seven-thirty in the morning, he died.

We had a small service. Then I drove home to Cal and the babies.

I will not, and in any case cannot, describe what I felt on that drive. I will just say that I knew that my father had heard me as I sat with him. My abiding sense of being alone—cosmically alone—is, I now know, a direct result of my own parents' savage divorce, coupled with my father's alcoholism. How else could the parent with whom you were so closely bonded simply disappear, to be replaced by this Darth Vader figure? The only answer, in my addled little psyche, had been that love is *not* real. We are *not* actually bonded to one another; love does *not* actually make a stitch in the fabric of the universe. It seems to do so for a time, but it can be ripped out when you least expect it. The cosmic needle coldly moves on to thread together another panel. You are left alone, strings hanging out, fluttering off into the dark. Cal had changed this for me. Until my children were born, my connection to Cal was the closest I'd ever come to feeling what it must feel like to experience a miracle. I do not mean this in any maudlin or fuzzy way. I mean it actually. And I knew that my father needed me to be with him as he left life. I knew that my dad loved me, in spite of everything.

The night I came home from my father's house, I turned to Cal in bed as he was reading. I felt an overwhelming urge to bind with him, to lock souls. Thank God, I said, we didn't have to suffer like my father. Thank God we weren't alone! He turned to me, nodded, and then kept reading. I waited, thinking he was finishing a paragraph.

But I ended up falling asleep. For days, weeks—nothing. I went numb. A few months later, I got a serious case of pneumonia, which lasted nearly twelve weeks. I spent a lot of time on the couch, in and out of blackout sleep, with my children coming to hang out and read with me, Cal watching TV. Wow. *He's really gone,* I remember thinking at one point. *We* are *alone.*

SEVEN

EVERYTHING IS COMING TO A GRINDING HALT:
THE END OF THE MARRIAGE

The arc of my life story tracks that of many in my generation; I'm a dime a dozen. But in the particulars of the dissolution of my own marriage, I am—everyone is—unique. By the end of my marriage, I had given up trying to do anything in the kitchen and had not washed a dish in a year. Cal had not been able to "find time" to read the book I had written, and he was explosive at any disclosure of my confusion or hurt. We rarely spoke, except about logistics. We hadn't had sex in months.

Yet I never considered divorce. It never even entered my mind. I just figured that this was my life. I was, by and large, okay with it. At this point, I had a number of good friends—many of them other mothers in our neighborhood—and that comfy camaraderie provided a soft lining. I had found a resting place for my adolescent mania: I loved my babies. *Loved* my babies. I was grateful that they had a perfect father, for our family meals, for the stability of our home, for neighborhood playdates.

Still, I felt it. *The ogre will come in any case.* I was beginning to feel it at night in the girls' room when I was still awake with a boo-boo snoring sweetly at each side. During the day, I was content with work, children, playdates, laundry. But once the sun set, my mind froze in panic. Grendel, it seemed, was just beyond the fortress gates, waiting for everyone to fall asleep.

I had to stay alert; I had to get us out. I instantly picked up my pace. But out of *where*? To what? Rather than progressing in any one direction, I manically pitched myself this way and that—like a metronome with no weight on its pendulum. Move, move, *move*.

Maybe our apartment was too small. The girls were getting bigger. The rooms were tiny; the "nests" were more like pods. We needed more space. We should move to a real house. I had grown up in a house, until my parents divorced; Cal had always grown up in a house. The girls deserved to grow up in a house, too. We should buy a house. Now was the time to do it; our apartment had appreciated, thanks to the kitchen renovation. We could sell our place for double what we paid for it. Think about it. We could afford a *house* now— not in the Jersey suburbs, not in some shitbag Brooklyn dump! A *nice* house, in *our* neighborhood!

This time, it wasn't Cal who churned frenetically about real estate; it was me. My dad was dead. I had recovered from pneumonia. My book had been published. Now I had time. I searched for a house every moment I had free. What was I doing? I was moving. I was thinking literally. House hunting was not symbolic. We *needed* to get out of the apartment; we did not *fit* there; *that's* what was wrong. I *needed* to find a house. More than that, I needed to find *The House*—like The Magnolia Tree.

Room. Poems. Gash. Sleepwalking. Stars. Ice. Dad. House.

The House would protect us.

During the summer before we separated, Cal and I sold our perfect little apartment. We'd always hallucinated about buying a house, but we knew we'd never actually be able to afford one—never mind one of those classic early-1900s four-story Brooklyn beauties made famous by *Moonstruck*. But somehow, we had done it. For one thing, we'd gotten tapped by good real estate karma during the housing bubble, and we *were* able to sell our apartment for double what we'd paid for it five years earlier. I found a beautiful fixer-upper for well under market value. It was an estate sale, and the seller had cheaped out by opting to go with a schlubby local realtor rather than one of the carnivorous Manhattan-based firms. With no advertising in *The New York Times*, the house was flying under the radar; I swooped by, and we snatched it up. For another thing, we'd done pretty well financially, especially considering that both of us worked from home and arranged our work hours to fit our kids' schedules. We had made it—again.

The day we closed on that house, I cried: *This is the place where we are going to raise our children until they go to college. It will be their childhood Home.* Having moved again and again as a kid following my parents' divorce, this was a huge, huge deal to me. It was the big door prize. With a jumbo mortgage in our pocket, we poured everything we had left into a gut renovation of that house. We hired a contractor to update its foundation and infrastructure, an architect to help preserve its period feeling. We installed new steel I-beams to bolster the century-old building. We updated all the electrical wiring and plumbing; installed new walls, closets, and floors; mounted antique lighting fixtures, claw-foot tubs, and pedestal sinks. We modified the floor plan to make the first floor a separate apartment, which we would rent out to cushion our monthly mortgage payments. Everything was figured out. We had made it.

That summer, as the contractors ripped out the innards of the old house and erected in their place a skeleton of steel beams, we stayed with Cal's parents again. We slept in separate bedrooms. Cal's parents urged us to go out together; they'd be happy to watch the kids. I'd look at Cal; he'd shrug. He never took them up on it. The demolition wore on, and our stay extended to autumn. Cal's mother grew insistent: Take a *break*! *Enjoy*! *Anak,* Cal—why are you so antiso*cial*? *Ano,* take your wife *out*! Thus pushed, Cal could not refuse. So, that November evening, we finally went out alone. I don't think that either of us knew what was coming. But it came in any case.

"Oh, do not ask, 'What is it?' / Let us go and make our visit." There it is—the old standard poem of high school English class, T. S. Eliot's *The Love Song of J. Alfred Prufrock*. Prufrock. He sits in the mind as a neutered Edwardian bachelor, the turn-of-the-twentieth-century Modern Man yearning to find meaning in a mannered world. But these days, he is considered an anachronism. You do not expect to see J. Alfred Prufrock sitting across the table from you at dinner, alive in the aspect of a twenty-first-century Generation X husband and father. You do not expect him to have seen the moment of his greatness flicker, to have seen the eternal Footman hold his coat and snicker, in short, to have been afraid. You do not expect him to be sitting across from you in a LOVE KILLS Ed Hardy sweatshirt wrestling with those selfsame quietly desperate, punishing questions.

We had wanted to go to this restaurant since it had first opened, nearly four years before. And there we were, at our first dinner out alone together in close to a year. The weight of it was so great that I broke down. I said, after our appetizers had been cleared away, that I thought we should look into seeing a couples therapist, that something needed to change. I did not see that this would be his moment. But it was, though I don't believe he knew it until it was right in front of him. It was his moment. He pushed it to its crisis. "We should have broken up ten years ago," he said coldly. "I've been completely fucking miserable; I have nothing to look forward to; I don't want to wake up at fifty and be in the same place. I'm *done.*"

He was not Prufrock. He was not my father. He was not my mother. He was not my husband. *He didn't want to.*

It was over.

We drove back to his parents' house. He went into one bedroom, I went into the other. The next day, I was aware of every speck of dust, flicker of light; nothing else seemed real. In hindsight, this was the most real moment of all. Why didn't we *stop right there*—figure out a way to patch things up? This is the most painful question of all. It is still the only one to which I do not have an answer I can articulate. All I can report is that it was as if a cosmic force had been unleashed, and in that instant—the instant in which Cal said "I'm done"—the finality of it roared in like an enormous black cloud blotting out the sky, over every inch of the world. It was done.

But then, one of the first things that you find yourself doing in the immediate aftermath of a disaster is thinking logistically. And you think strangely fast, making quick, practical decisions that you believe, in your revved-up mind, will help resurrect order. Cal and I went from barely talking to speaking in businesslike terms, ticking off agenda items. First, we will move into the house, we said; we will not tell the children anything. So, a few weeks after our dinner conversation, we did that. Then we were in the house. Cal would sleep on the sofa until the apartment downstairs was ready. Since we hadn't slept in the same room for years, we reasoned, this would not strike our children as the end of the world. We would not tell them that the plan was for him to move into the downstairs apartment, not yet. We would discuss that when it came up. But they knew something was bad. We climbed into bed one night, and as we were snuggling to sleep, my younger daughter whispered: "I'm scared of our house—it has ghosts."

One of the things I have always despised so intensely about Baby Boomers and their divorces was how breathtakingly egocentric they were. That they were so eager to trade in their children's very sense of safety in the world for access to an unfettered sex life and a sense of "personal fulfillment" was so shocking and brutal to me that I have to storm out of the room whenever I hear some self-aggrandizing asshole talking about it. The cognitive dissonance is nauseating.

The few times I was invited to visit him, my father used to sit in the "family room" of the suburban McMansion he'd built for his wife and four stepchildren—scotch in hand—lecturing me about how important it was to be true to oneself, not to be tethered by others' expectations, to just say "fuck it" and "do it"—that this was the path to happiness. And I'd be thinking: Monster. How can you possibly sit there, looking at your thirteen-year-old daughter who misses you so consumingly, with her little shaved head and ripped black punk uniform, who sends you bad poems slashed with grief and fear, and say you're walking along the road of happiness? Is your heart a lump of charred charcoal? Are you even human anymore?

Cut to—me, age thirty-eight, front seat of the brand-new BMW that Cal and I have decided to go halvesies on since we still need a car for the kids, and we both are shamefacedly fond of good driving cars. Zanny is in the backseat, and we are listening to the Pixies. I turn down the music and tell her I've noticed that she's been really angry lately; would she like to talk about it? She asks why Daddy is sleeping on the sofa. When we come to a stoplight, my voice says that though it is hard to understand that Mama and Daddy have a grown-up relationship that is different from our being her and her sister's parents, we do, and we need a little space from each other: a time-out of sorts. She starts to weep and asks if that means we're getting a divorce. It is now raining. Because it is a fancy new car, the windshield wipers come on automatically. *We're not talking about divorce now, my baby,* the voice says. *This is grown-up stuff, and Daddy and I are working on it, but we love you, and because we love you, we will always be a family. We will always know how to take care of you.* She wails: *Please tell me if you are going to get divorced before it happens, so I won't be surprised, okay Mama?* I'm thinking: *What the hell am I doing? Who the fuck am I? How can I be saying this shit to my beautiful daughter, my firstborn? What am I doing? What am I doing?*

What am I doing? The only thing that mattered was the kids. We had not yet told our children that we were separating, much less divorcing, because we had not figured out what we were going to do, logistically. We said to each other that we didn't want to traumatize them with frightening terms until we could all get used to what "separation" and "divorce" would actually feel like to the four of us on a day-to-day, rhythmic basis. We said to each other that we wanted to do everything possible to make sure that our children were not feeling the impact of what we were feeling. What were we feeling? What was happening? *What am I doing? What am I doing?*

Early in our separation, I was up in my room, on the floor, rocking on my knees, guttural and howling. I heard the downstairs door open and my children and husband walk in. I panicked, listening to them scampering up the stairs to me: *Get it together, Susie.* I pressed my forehead into the floor, and the door flung open. "What are you doing, Mama?" I heard my little one ask. "Hold on a sec, guys, I'm just finishing up a little yoga," I said, head still down, trying to buy myself a few more seconds. "Let's go wash hands, and then we'll get a little ice cream, and you can tell me about your day." More scampering, into the bathroom. I raised my head, wiped my face, shook my head, and pinched my cheeks. "Okay!" I called. "Ready?"

What am I doing? Everything was happening so fast. One of the things I knew we were *not* going to do was to sit down and have the Important Family Announcement. Cal said: *Fine.* From my point of view, the big thing was for our guys to feel secure that both of us absolutely loved them, beyond a shadow of a doubt. If there was no modulation in that sense, they would be generally okay. The little girls would pad around in their footie PJs, getting books ready for bedtime, and just kiss their dad goodnight, unworried that he would be leaving for the night to go sleep with a friend. Then the three of us would crawl into bed, read, and snuggle as we always had.

The problems seemed to come when there *was* modulation,

which was hard to avoid when we were distracted or angry—which is pretty much the milieu of divorce. That is, if he hesitated at all before leaving—or indicated that he would rather not be leaving—that was it. The children would collapse in tears on the sofa, clinging to him desperately. I wanted to kill him for involving them in his feelings. They were so sad I almost couldn't look at them. This was exactly why I never wanted to get divorced. *What am I doing?*

One night, on the eve of his returning from a month-long trip early in our separation, I had a hysterical crying fit. I hadn't realized how anxious I was about his coming back, about separating at all, about anything, really—and I just lost it. I couldn't stop crying. In front of my guys. They stared at me, then tried to comfort me by bringing me toilet paper and rubbing my back. My boo-boos. I couldn't believe I was doing this to them, this Medea tantrum. I tried to apologize, but it was useless, I knew. I had done exactly what I never, ever wanted to do.

Neither Cal nor I could imagine him living outside the house. The idea that our children would think that he left was unbearable to both of us. *What am I doing?* But I could not stand the sight of him on the sofa watching TV. I wondered if he would end up being a dick about money, like my father, who had, I later found out, died with a warrant out for his arrest in Norristown, Pennsylvania, for failure to pay my mother outstanding child support. Was this Cal? Where was *Cal?* What was happening? *What am I doing?*

What was happening was inconceivable. People think you have discernible feelings right after something like this happens. I did not. I only knew that it was happening, and it was happening faster than I could process it. Cal's and my conversations were quick, efficient meetings. We had reached the point, we said, at which it is appropriate to tell the children that something bigger is happening. But not too big. We should do this gradually, we said, so that nothing like the Important Family Announcement drops like a bomb on them. Small steps, we said, small steps. So we took the next one. We said that, as they had probably noticed, Mama and Daddy had been pretty grumpy with each other lately, and that we had decided to have a time-out from each other. They were concerned and fearful, wanted to know how long this time-out was going to last. We said that we didn't know; we were just going to see how it went, until we had a little space to ourselves to calm down. Mama and Daddy had an adult relationship, and we were taking care of it. We loved them, and we were always there to take care of them.

But after Cal moved into the apartment, we both erupted, though we disguised our feelings in the children's presence. Although the living situation provided an essential sense of continuum and stability for the children—and I'd do it the same way again in a second because of that—it quickly devolved into hateful late-night texting tirades. It was a torrent. Every drop of poison that we'd choked back for years—verging on two decades—came vomiting out of each of us, almost involuntarily. I had never loved *him,* he spat; I only loved that he took *care* of me! Frankly, when he thought about it, how well did I really even *know* him? Did I know what he dreamed about, what he wished he had done with his life? Had I ever even see him for who he *was?* I was just like my *father*—I *used* people, then I threw them away.

I shrieked in literal agony when I read this. Was this *true?* Was I a black-hearted narcissist? What had I done? After sitting with this for several days, however, it occurred to me: How could *everything* be my fault? For the last seven years, I had assumed blame for everything because I really did think that everything *was* my fault and that Cal was perfect. I realized: Cal had not disabused me of this perception. Not once.

That's when I became livid. You have been *taking advantage* of my guilt and my shitty self-esteem to hide from your*self!* I lashed back. How can you say that *I* am throwing *you* away when I have worked for seven years to right my wrongs? *You* have ground me into the asphalt, *you* have made me feel worthless, *you* have rejected my every gesture at closeness because *you* do not want *anyone* to know you! If *I* am my father's *daughter,* then *you* are his ill-begotten *son.*

A détente ensued. The eruption, though furious, was weirdly purifying. Cal and I both seemed to sense that in it we had come up against something hard and real. In the final analysis, the truth was that neither had Cal been revolving around me nor I around him. We were both solitary entities revolving around a star that was finally dying.

EIGHT

THE CUTTER:
SEPARATION

In the immediate aftershock following a bomb going off, everything goes flat, noiseless, vacant. This sounds dramatic. It didn't feel that way. It just felt like what reality actually is. It had been here, undergirding everything, all along. There was a vibratory quality to it. If "Om" is the rich, living sound of the universe, the sound of this place was its polar opposite. If there can be such a thing, it was the vibration of nothing at all. This was not unfamiliar terrain for me. I lived there for many years after my own parents' divorce. I lived there for much of the year following our separation. But after the flat, white-noise period, cracks appeared, as if the land was just now responding to the blast.

About three months into the separation, an abyss began to open up in front of me. I didn't see it coming. But I felt it, and the wider I felt it opening, the more I became convinced that in fact it had always been there, it was all around me, and it was never going to close. Let me be clear that this is not a metaphor. The pitch and depth of this void—I felt it, palpably, all the time. After it had been with me for about a month, unabating, I started to think that maybe the seismic impact set off by my marital rupture had blown open the door to some higher reality for me. You hear of people who say that following an operation, accident, or some other major trauma, they were instantaneously endowed with the sense datum of collective purpose, universal light. In my case, the blunt force of trauma had blasted open this abyss. It was *my* ultimate reality.

I didn't know what to do. In spite of my other nasty experiences earlier in life, I had no experience with this. I was aware that I was losing it. But I was already doing everything that everybody tells you to do. I was already in therapy. I was already on antidepressants. I was already doing yoga. I was already eating right. Still, it was there. When I was alone, it was just the void. When I ventured out into the world or was with other people, however, it took on an almost malevolent quality. It was like being a character in a Stephen King short story. Your workaday life is mundane; you look okay to people. It's simply that wherever you go, an invisible grotesque presence is three steps behind you. There is no question of shaking it. Sometimes it speeds closer, its breath at your cheek; other times it lags. It has been there all along; you just see it now. The question was not how I could make it go away, but rather whether it was worth it to walk with it at all.

One crystalline day in February, I sat in my car underneath the Brooklyn Bridge. I got out. I looked up. For a while. I got back in. My babies.

The only time I felt okay was when I was with them, transported back to the world in which I was the mom with her schmushkies. I was able to make dinner, sing loudly, and dance, which are normal mom things to my children. But the way Cal and I had decided to arrange things—trying out joint custody—I was without my children half the time.

Because I didn't know what else to do, I met with the minister of the church I attended intermittently. Since Zanny's birth, I had come to a relatively comfortable meeting place with God, especially in my conversations with my children. It was always cast in the rubric of love. When we were mad and struck out, we had a talk about how we were ignoring God for the moment. But we could always go back, and when we did, we felt better because then our hearts were restored to normal. When we talked about life after death, we said that there is nothing to be afraid of. Our bodies were our bodies, and they were good and useful while we were alive, but the bigger deal is that we had always been together, and we always would be. And these things felt real and authentic because I just knew, in my gut, that it was the truth. Especially after my dad died.

Now, however, I wasn't sure about anything I had thought before. Sitting in the minister's living room, I told him, frankly, that I didn't know what else to do but pray for help and that I wasn't sure how to do that. He sat quietly for a moment and then prescribed to me *lectio divina*, Latin for "holy reading." He explained that this form of prayer dated back to the twelfth century and was intended to be a feasting on the Word (making it, he said, a particularly fitting form of prayer for writers and talky people in general). It is composed of four sequential parts, he said: *lectio*, in which one reads a scriptural passage slowly and attentively, not so much for comprehension as for grace and beauty; *meditatio*, in which the Holy Spirit working within you will illuminate—actually light up—a particular phrase in the scripture; *oratio*, in which one lets this phrase roll over and repeat itself internally, and in so doing, enters into intuitive conversation with God; and finally *contemplatio*, simple, loving comfort in God—joyful rest. He instructed me to start with the Psalms, to open to any page and just begin. *Make sure you set aside at least an hour to do this,* he said, *and try to do it at the same time each day.*

Oh, I thought. I didn't really know what I had been expecting from my visit. But as I left the parsonage, the black weight pulled down on me with new force. I think I had almost hoped he would do something magical, like a laying on of hands: to touch my forehead and relieve me with some kind of surprising, special blessing. There hadn't been any miracle. Ridiculous.

I waved politely to the minister and pulled the door closed behind me. It was a clear late February afternoon. The streets were bright, antiseptic—a study in physics, light refracting off every plane. As my eyes adjusted, I felt it materialize: The demon I'd deposited at the threshold was exactly where I'd left it.

I was not looking forward to night.

But night came. I read my children several books and lay down with them until they fell asleep, as I always did. Although I often ended up falling asleep with them and would have been happy to do that on this night, I was wide awake. There was nothing for me to do but go into my room and sit on my bed, eyes open. I knew I wouldn't be able to do anything but that, and I didn't want to do that. But lying between my kids with this black *thing* clinging to my chest felt wrong, as though I was letting a monster into their room. So I got up.

I sat on the bed in my room. When we were renovating the house, we had decided that our bedroom would be painted a meditative blue, with nothing hanging on the walls to busy it. Now, contemplative quietude was cold space. My gaze drifted over to the stacks of books, which I hadn't bothered to organize, lined up against the baseboards. I didn't want to read any of them. They were mostly giveaways that my mother had just cleared out from her own house to make room for a move to a condo—outdated feminist literary criticism, the lesser works of John Dos Passos and Upton Sinclair, coffee table books on Modern chair design and the plight of Venice. There were two cards posted on my mirror. One was from my agent and friend, Tina. It had arrived paper-clipped to a check for a thousand dollars and a note: "Don't say anything—just cash it." I ripped up the check and taped up the note. Another was a homemade Valentine from my friend Heather. She had drawn a heart and written in the middle of it: "You are here."

But as I was looking away, my eye landed on the giant Bible, with its gilded pages and medieval art, that Pru had given me for Christmas that year. She had been very excited, and proud of her present. She had chosen it for me because, she said, "You like God, Mama." When I'd said I guessed that was true but wondered what in particular had made her think so, she explained, "You like church, and I don't really, but I also just know that you like God." Bunny rabbit. It is hackneyed to say that your children pick up more on what you do than on what you say you do, but it is nonetheless true. I guess I had inserted the whole idea of God into my children's lives a lot more than maybe I'd realized. That made me glad. Yet there was my baby's Holy Bible, and there I was on the bed thinking about what she, with her little mammal face, had said to me. And I was thinking that I had pushed the whole God thing precipitously. Or maybe not precipitously, just stupidly, desperately. I had made it up to make myself and my children feel better. Of course, I loved my children, I loved my children. And in some ways, I could muster up the idea that there was something Greater for them. But I could not muster it up for myself. It wasn't real. This void was real. It had always been real. My heart wasn't ice. It was dust.

I sat there for a long time.

At some point, I just opened it up. I don't know what hour of night or early morning it was; it was very dark out. I didn't decide *I am going to do this now,* nor did I feel some force compelling me to open it—nothing like that. It's just that one moment I was not doing something, and the next I was. I happened to flip to Psalm 60.

O God, thou hast cast us off, thou hast scattered us,
  thou hast been displeased; O turn thyself to us again.
Thou hast made the earth to tremble; thou hast broken
  it: heal the breaches thereof; for it shaketh.

I did begin to feel something, reading this.

Thou hast shewed thy people hard things: thou hast
  made us to drink the wine of astonishment.

Reading on was too much. What had been black and static now roiled. I could not read it.

But then I got to it. It didn't light up on the page, as the prescription of *lectio divina* had described that it might. I can't explain it except to say that I came through something and got to it.

Who will bring me into the strong city?

I lifted my head. I closed the book. I sat.

After a long time, I realized that I was not just sitting anymore. I felt light.

One of the outcomes of practicing *lectio divina* is that it compelled me to read the Bible regularly. Frankly, I'd never really gotten much out of the Bible. Everyone says how wonderful its language is, how powerful its imagery is, how central a knowledge of it is to a basic understanding of Western literature and philosophy. The latter is incontestable, but as for the rest, I don't know—not so much, for me anyway. It's not that I didn't like the people in it. I love Moses and Jacob: all their conflicts, tantrums, and doubts. And Jesus, to me, is the very definition of hard-core punk. Indeed, my first tattoo, at age nineteen, was a Jesus fish because my friend Nate and I had decided that—as the primitive password of the early, persecuted Christians—

it was *the* most powerful symbol of rebellion of all time. But the Bible itself? It's not at all smart, sensitive, or educated of me, but I always found the language arcane and autocratic, the imagery obvious. I read the Bible so that I could read Donne, Dante, Spenser, and Shakespeare, but I used it primarily as a reference book. I once even got a bit of a thrashing from an assistant philosophy professor at Columbia when I was sophomorically critiquing something about symbolism in the Bible's literary style in a paper. He actually called me into his office and put it to me point-blank: "Do you not appreciate that for millions of people, the Bible is a sacred text?" I realized later that he was basically telling me not to be such an asshole—that for most of the people who read it, it isn't symbolic—but at the time, I was shocked. *Is he crazy?* I remember thinking. *God, how'd a rube like that get a gig teaching here?*

Coming to the Bible with nothing left was different. I have heard people talk about the "gift of desperation," which sounds to me like junky New Age self-help twaddle (as does any phrase invoking "gift"). While I still bristle at it, I now understand this expression. Moreover, it was precisely the desperation in the biblical voices of David, Solomon, Jeremiah, Job that helped. It isn't the vernacular of contemporary depression and angst, does not evoke a vocabulary that includes "good boundaries," "owning" this or that feeling, or "taking care of" oneself. It is the language of flat-out despair. It is that of Lear on the heath, of Macduff after he learns that Macbeth's henchmen have slaughtered his wife and all his children: "All my pretty ones? / Did you say all? O hell-kite! All? / What, all my pretty chickens and their dam / At one fell swoop?"* This is the kind of language that I understood.

I understood the imagery of physical mortification. To someone in despair, this imagery is not symbolic; it is the thing itself. Before my father died, I had not understood this. Being with him in his last twelve hours of life, watching him actually die, holding his cold,

* *Macbeth,* Act IV, scene iii.

swollen hand, changed that. It is a luxury of inexperience to think in metaphors; death is death is death. What's more, I had always been very proud of my "tough as nails" status; I could power through anything, and often had. But my physical response in the days and weeks after my father's death cut me off at the knees. A cold became a three-month case of pneumonia. I just couldn't get better. I sustained permanent lung damage. I'd never been sick like that, ever; now I carry around an inhaler.

I started to practice *lectio divina* every night after my children went to sleep. It became my favorite time of day. It made me feel as if I was not alone.

I would sit there at first, blackness palpably pressing at my head, shoulders, and stomach, and I would start reading. As I did, a lambent warmth would seep in, through my forehead and then just above my stomach. I could also see it, in the proverbial mind's eye, glowy and solar. Reading a psalm, I felt it swelling to the extent that I was almost buoyant in it. It was good, almost essential, to have that floaty sense of incubation, because when the *meditatio* phase moved in—the part in which a phrase lights up—the lines that ebbed in my mind during *oratio* were hard. Lovely, but sharp-edged, like glinting diamonds.

> God is in the middle of her; she shall not be moved.
>
> *Psalm 46*
>
> Behold, you desire truth in the inward parts.
>
> *Psalm 51*
>
> Make me to hear joy and gladness; that the bones
>   which you have broken may rejoice.
>
> *Ibid.*

In the end, *contemplatio*. Rest. I needed it. I would continue to need it.

———

In the late spring, just eight months after we had bought it, we put our house on the market. As word of our separation spread, the cozy, familiar neighborhood in which we had lived, in three different places over nearly a decade and a half—longer than I'd ever lived anywhere in my life—had become bare and mean, like a savanna. I could not walk down the street without bumping into another mother of young children, who wanted to know how I was "doing." Except for a few friends, I could sense something hyenalike as they stared into me. I felt as though I was being watched, a wounded animal about to be separated from the pack. Or at least that's how it seemed. It would have been difficult for it not to have.

When I left Park Slope, I moved into an apartment above a vacant Laundromat in a neighborhood whose streets I'd been scared to walk down just five years earlier. When a vagrant, mute alcoholic moved into the abandoned storefront with the permission of the landlord, I could no longer have my children stay there safely. I told Cal that we should explain to them that the apartment was too uncomfortable, too hot—better to wait until Mama found a really good place to live. *Okay,* Cal said, *sounds good.*

I saw Zanny and Pru every day. We went to free public beaches. Often, I didn't even have enough money to buy them Popsicles, a dollar apiece.

By midsummer I was broke. I wasn't just running low—I was bankrupt. I had put everything into our house, in cash. I had some savings left from a mutual fund, but I ran through it by August and was looking for quarters under the sofa. It never occurred to me to ask for financial help from Cal. I had always made my share of money; we were equal partners. But I had no work; even if I had been offered it, I'm not certain that I could have done it. For the first time in my life, my grit vanished. I was lost.

There was some physical disintegration. I vomited intermittently. I didn't tell anyone about it, didn't go to the doctor. I got used to it.

My hair started to come out in clumps. Then, I became infested, and reinfested, with head lice. After the fourth bout, I cut off my hair and bleached it within an inch of its life. Combined with my weight loss, I looked eerily as I had as a teenager.

Nearly a decade after I'd quit, I started smoking again.

Pink welts burst open all over my body. They itched and itched. I clawed at my skin until my stomach, arms, and legs were rutted with scabs. Ultimately, I had to go to the emergency room. When the registering nurse asked me for my name, I said, "Job." She looked at me. "Name," she said. I was given Benadryl and steroid shots for stress hives. In the examining room, the doctor asked me if I had been subject to domestic abuse.

I stuttered.

I kept the light on all night long. I couldn't read a book. I didn't have a TV. I knitted a lot. I continued *lectio divina,* but often, it was hard to concentrate. Often, I gave up and sat.

My babies. It had been a huge mistake to bleach my hair, the lice notwithstanding. The change in hair, the change in weight, the scabs patched over my skin. To children, mother's body is home. Now my body was different. After all the home improvements that Cal and I had insisted were necessary to provide our children a homey home, only to watch as those "improvements" destroyed our family anyway, I had done something even more devastating to my babies' sense of home: I had done a gut job on my own body. The only thing I could do was to reassure them that it would return to the way it was very soon, that things were unsettled right now; once they settled, my hair, body, everything, would, too. I was still Mama, and they were still the schmushkies. This was a hard time, but it wouldn't be hard forever. My children. What could I say? When I was with them, during the day, I was fine. I was myself, they were themselves; we did Mama and Zanny and Pru things. *What was I doing?*

I could not be with other people. When you are in this kind of desolation, people become afraid of you. Even if you are doing a decent job of disguising your feelings, they can still see what's happening physically. It is frightening to them. Friends said they wanted to come visit, to help. Few did. I understood this.

> I was a derision to all my people; and their song all the
>   day.
> He hath filled me with bitterness, he hath made me
>   drunken with wormwood.
> He hath also broken my teeth with gravel stones, he
>   hath covered me with ashes.
> And thou hast removed my soul far off from peace: I
>   forgat prosperity.*

There was a hallucinatory quality to all this. I did not understand where I was. At night it was the worst, because I was not with my children. I was not where I lived. I was not with Cal and my babies, in our cozy, gemlike apartment. I was not there. I was here, in this hollow apartment in Red Hook, with its broken door and fluorescent lights and no phone, its mattress on the floor, its vagrant drunk outside the window, terrors, terrors. I could not understand where I was. *Where were my children? Why weren't my children here? What was I doing?*

Alone. I was alone.

---

* The Book of Lamentations (King James Bible), III, xiv–xvii.

—◆◆▶✕◀◆◆—

NINE

LEVITATE ME:
DIVORCE AND DENOUEMENT

One morning, at the end of that summer, I woke up and thought: *Mom.*

I had not seen my mother since early spring, when she and Joseph had come to see Zanny and Pru. It had been five months. A lot had happened in these five months. I wanted to be with my mother.

I knew that she would be in Maine, at the family's old vacation place. I called and asked her if it would be okay if I came with Zanny and Pru. "Of *course*, Pickle," she said. "Just get in the car and come right now." So I picked up the girls from Cal, and we went. We arrived late that evening. The next day, while the girls were down at the beach playing with Joseph, Mom and I sat on the porch, and I knit frantically. It was the first time that my mother had seen me scabby, wasted. "Oh, my darling," she said, trembling. "I had no idea how bad things had gotten." I put down my knitting and saw my bitten hands. "Yes," I said.

Later that night, after the children had gone to sleep, my stepfather said to me: "Dear, why didn't you tell us?" My mother and stepfather would transfer money into my bank account. They would lend me the old station wagon that they had planned on selling. I looked up at them standing in front of me, Joseph's arm enfolding Mom's shoulder.

One day after lunch, Zanny and Pru and I decided to row from our beach to the end of a nearby point and back. We zipped up our life preservers and set off. But the farther I rowed, the more it became clear that I had misjudged the distance, and by the time we reached the point, my arms were locked stiff in spasms; I had rowed almost five miles. I dragged the boat up onto the beach and flopped down, while the girls helped themselves delightedly to the beach's treasure chest of sea urchins and sand dollars. It was going to start getting dark in about an hour or so. I couldn't believe how irresponsible and reckless I was. What the hell was I *thinking*? I should have turned around after the first mile, but I'd persisted, sure that the point was going to be around the next bend. Now, I could barely move. How was I going to make it?

Who knows whether, as many world cultures believe, one's ancestors appear with mysterious gestures of help at critical times. But as I was sitting there, I felt my dad. I did not "hear" him but rather *sensed* him saying, "Come on, Suze-o! Piece of cake—tough as nails!" I broke into a huge grin. Then I got up. "Okay, baby rabbits, back in the boat!" I called. "We've got to get back in time for dinner!" The row back was *hard*, and while I did not let on to the girls that I was genuinely scared for our safety, I definitely cursed and howled for a good ten minutes, and then we started singing songs to keep the rowing rhythm going—and, really, just for fun.

Somewhere, about halfway along, Pru yelled: "Dolphins!" We looked, and on the seaward side of our boat, there were three gray porpoises looping in and out of the black water. "It's a mommy dolphin and her children, right, Mama?" cried Pru excitedly. "You don't *know* that," said Zanny. "It could be a *daddy* or just three *grown-ups.*" I rolled my eyes. "Whoever they are, they're *awesome,*" I said. Zanny giggled. The porpoises continued to lap alongside us, and we watched them as we slowly heaved forward with every stroke. "But you know what, Mama?" said Zanny. "I think they're trying to make sure we get home okay, don't you think so?" It did look that way. The threesome accompanied us right to the cove of our little beach, then undulated away.

We waved and cheered to them as we pulled in to shore. Pru hopped out onto the rocky beach and went tearing up the meadow to the house, shouting at the top of her lungs so that Mom and Joseph would hear her, "Dolphins! Dolphins! Dolphins!" I pulled the boat up, and then Zanny and I started making our way through the meadow. "I can't believe you rowed so far, Mama," she said. "You're *strong.*" I gave her a smushy hug. "Everybody had a job—you guys did the singing and talking, and I did the rowing, right?" I said. "We're a pretty scrappy crew, huh?" Zanny nodded. "It was nice of the dolphins, too," she said.

That evening, as I was trying to put the girls to bed, my mother kept on intruding with more and more stories about Odysseus and Scylla and Charybdis and Circe and various plot turns in *The Odyssey* to which she wanted to compare us and our afternoon adventure. The girls and I were exhausted, and we just wanted to sleep.

"*Ma!*" I shouted. "Stop! Please!" My mother stopped on a dime, her eyes wide, and she held up one finger as she reached in her pocket with the other hand, rummaging for something.

"What are you *doing*?" I moaned. She produced from her pocket a stack of thick white business cards and handed them to me.

"I forgot to give these to you earlier, and I just want you to look at them right now," she said.

"I will look at them in the morning, Mom—we have to *sleep,*" I pleaded.

"It will take you *less* than a moment—just look at them, and then I'll go away." I sighed self-pityingly and looked at one of the cards. Engraved in a refined Tiffany's typeface were two words: STOP TALKING. I looked up at my mom. She smiled impishly.

"The idea here is that you, Joseph, Zanny, and Pru are to hand me one of these cards should I become too effusive, all right?" she said. "Now, off to bed with you all, intrepid swashbucklers!" I laughed so hard that I did, for the first time, actually lose command of my bladder. As I ran to the bathroom, Mom tucked the girls in, and when I returned, she hugged me fiercely.

"You're a hell of a mother, Susie," she whispered. "These little girls are so well loved, and they are going to be *fine*." I looked at her and beamed. No metaphors: This was just *my* mother encouraging *her* granddaughters and *me*. I hugged her back. Fiercely.

When we got back from Maine, I started to come out of isolation. Wonderful things began happening. Sometimes, said Truman Capote, there is a God. Every day, it seemed, was that sometimes.

My godmother called me. "Susie, dear," she announced, "we are going out for lunch at Bergdorf's." Sitting there with my ragged hair, I ate the lobster salad with citrus vinaigrette. I smiled at my godmother. She smelled so marvelous, her signature eyeglasses were so chic, she sounded so wonderful.

One day, I called up my dear friend Judith. She didn't know who it was at first. When I repeated myself, she laughed. Then she started sobbing. "Oh, Susie!" she cried. "I'm sorry—I'm just so happy to hear your voice!"

Ian began pinging me on g-chat several times a day, sending annoying greetings like "Hola!" and "Hey, big mama!" and directing me to stupid websites with videos of Japanese reality TV shows or telling me where to download old hardcore punk songs for free. I knew what he was doing. I love my brother.

My friend Barbara texted me: "I'm coming whether you like it or not." I couldn't have her in that apartment, so I met her at the nearby Ikea. We took the escalator up to the living room area, plopped down on a couch in one of the demo rooms, and made ourselves comfortable. We hung out there all day, talking. People ambled through the room and smiled uncertainly at us. We welcomed them, as if into our home.

After the house sold—the day before the housing bubble burst and the markets collapsed in 2008—I took my share and invested it in a little house, in that same Brooklyn neighborhood that I was scared to visit just five years ago, but in a safer part of it. It was what I could afford, but it was a disaster, full of carbon monoxide leaks and lead drinking-water pipes. I slept on the floor on a mat and cried every night. It was two months before my children could stay overnight there. I had to book cheapo rooms at the Comfort Inn in Brooklyn via Priceline to spend the night with them, charging it to a credit card that I pushed to its five-digit limit.

One time, I said screw it, fun was in order. I booked a discounted room at the Hilton in Times Square for five nights. Zanny, Pru, and I were tourists in our own city. At the box office where *Young Frankenstein,* the musical, was playing, the manager looked at the kids and me and said, "Tell you what—if you come to the matinee, I'll give you seventy-five percent off the tickets." So we went to see it (I was counting on their not getting the blue humor, and they didn't). We ate at the giant Dallas BBQ; the waiter gave us extra fries, on the house. That Sunday, we went to Saint John the Divine for the annual blessing of the animals. We took pictures as they trotted down the aisle: a donkey, a miniature camel, a wallaby. We ate Korean barbecue afterward and visited Columbia. "This is where Mama went to college," I said. "If you want to go here, you'd better start studying now, friends!" We all giggled. We went on a tour of Butler Library, roamed through the stacks, peeked in on the students hunched over in their carrels. All those *books.* All that work being worked on. My babies.

By and by, the house was repaired for safety. It did not have a working stove or fridge; there was no dishwasher. On autopilot, I went to the salesman at the fancy kitchen appliance emporium whom I'd befriended during the last two renovations in Park Slope. When I walked in, the first thing Ira said was: "Look at you, blondie!" The second thing he said was: "So, what—moving *again*? *Another* Wolf range now?" For some reason, it was too much: the absurdity, the assumption, the sadness. When I broke down, he sat me down and presented me with a box of tissues.

"Listen to me, doll," he said. "The same exact thing happened to me. Worst period of my life. But now, I'm happily remarried thirteen years—my kids have the best stepmother in the world!" He showed me his ring and then took hold of my hand. "You are going to be fine. Not for a while, but you are going to be *fine*." Forget the Wolf range and the crazy expensive fridge—*please*, you don't need that stuff—it's the home that counts, he said; your home is going to be beautiful because you and your kids will be in it. Then he gifted me with a ridiculous deal and waved me out. "Better than *fine*—you're not going to believe how great you'll be!"

A woman I'd always chatted with in Park Slope, where she owned an upscale home furnishings and clothing boutique, turned out to live in my new neighborhood. One day, she came by unannounced with giant shopping bags full of fancy scented candles, lovely hand-painted curtain panels, and linen tea towels. "You need things like this to feel good," she said in her fabulous Polish accent. After seeing the disaster afoot, she returned with stylish shelving and track lighting from her store. "You take them—they will look beautiful in your kitchen."

I didn't have anything to cook with. Cal had taken all the cookware and cookbooks with him, which was fair. But I had nothing, didn't know anything, and had no money for takeout. I got a set of pots and pans from Ikea for thirty bucks, went online for recipes, and started cooking. Because I had next to no money, I established two rules: (a) If it could be made, I would make it myself (meaning I made the bread, cereal, granola, cookies, cakes, cleaning products; no canned, presoftened beans, but dry ones that I soaked overnight; pizza, dough included; and so on); and (b) Dinner had to cost under ten dollars. We lived off the vegetables and herbs I planted in the garden. I did it. My children were amazed at first, but they came to expect it. Which pleased me beyond reason.

Cal didn't want the couches we had bought together, and they literally did not fit through the door to my tiny new house. But shortly after the house was ready for move-in, my mother called to say that my grandmother's house in Virginia needed to be cleared out. Nana, who had been staying in an assisted living home near my mother, was ninety-three, and it was time. None of the cousins wanted the furniture. Did I? That Thanksgiving, a year to the date of Cal's and my separation, I collected the furniture from my grandparents' three-hundred-year-old house in Middleburg, Virginia, where I had spent every Christmas after my parents divorced. Back in Brooklyn, our couches were the Victorian settees that once sat diplomats and heads of state in my great-grandparents' palatial apartment in Washington, D.C.; the Federal grandfather clock chimed every hour, just as it had in my grandparents' parlor; the quilts on our beds were stitched by my great-great-grandmothers and maiden aunts from Louisville, Kentucky. I made my children's room comfy and bedecked it with fairy lights and books. But the artwork was still the artwork, and my father's painting went center stage on the main wall. We moved in with our dog, parrot, four hamsters, and two hermit crabs. Zanny said to me, "You know what I love about our house? It's so *cozy*, even though it's usually messy. And when you don't look out the window, you feel as if you're in the forest."

In the forest. For the first year in that house, I would wake up in the middle of the night at least three times a week and not know where I was. Zanny and Pru, as if answering a beacon, would often groggily appear at my doorway and crawl into bed with me, and we would all fall back to sleep in a snuggly tangle.

When Cal and I agreed on a divorce settlement, we signed the papers in a Park Slope mediator's office. We had not disagreed about anything. We wanted joint custody, wanted the kids to stay as close to each of us as they always had been, wanted to talk regularly about the kids to keep each other up to date. We walked out of the office and onto the street. He was wearing a coat I'd never seen before. I looked at him. He looked past me. "Well," he said. "I guess that's that—take care of yourself, Susie." We shook hands. He got into his car, I got into my car.

A few minutes later, I broke down. I called him, sobbing: What *happened*? It was inevitable, he said. He should have known it that first year, when I moved to Washington. It was such an obvious sign. Cal chuckled caustically. Look, Susie, he said. I've obviously been doing a lot of thinking about everything, and I've come to the conclusion that everything we used to say about our souls being connected, that there was something written in the universe—that was all bullshit. It was something we said to rationalize why we were still together when we obviously shouldn't have been. We stayed together out of fear. If we had really paid attention to all those signs, we would have become friends a lot sooner and saved ourselves a lot of time that we ended up wasting. But we have the babies—and that's what counts.

Really? I said. You *really* mean that? Yes, he said. I do.

The first Christmas was a horror. The tree was too small, Zanny and Pru wailed. I knew it; I couldn't afford a bigger one. I had less than ten dollars in my bank account after buying it. I downloaded some free Christmas songs into my music player, perched it in its speaker apparatus, and brought up the Christmas ornaments and stockings from the basement. Zanny's stocking was nowhere to be found. I sat down on the couch.

"You know what?" I said. "I'm going to give you mine—the one I had as a little girl." Zanny took it, and I could see that she was happy to have it because it was special. But then she burst into tears.

"What are *you* going to use, Mama?" I would use the one that we'd gotten for Uncle Ian when he used to spend Christmases with us. I *liked* that one; it had bobolinks on it, which reminded me of Granddad.

"But it's not *yours*!" she cried. She lurched upstairs, sobbing. Pru and I stood in the living room, surrounded by the dusty cardboard boxes of ornaments.

"Are we still going to decorate the tree?" Pru asked. The instrumental theme to *A Charlie Brown Christmas* was playing. I looked at Pru. I shut my eyes for a beat, and then opened them. Little baby mammal. I smiled: Yes, we were *definitely* going to decorate the tree, but how about a little hot chocolate first?

"Yay!" cheered Pru. I poured cocoa into my grandmother's teacups; we sipped.

"Do you feel like this is a hard Christmas because things are so different?" I asked. Pru nodded, spooning around her drink. "I feel that way, too," I said.

"We already decorated our tree at Daddy's," she said. "It's *really* big—it's so beautiful, Mama." I asked her to tell me about it, and she described it in her widened-eyed, grand-gesturing, "magical world" way.

"It sounds *beautiful*, love," I said. "I bet it was so much fun to decorate it." She nodded that it was. "Our tree at Mama's will be beautiful, too, just different," she observed, shrugging. "It's okay that it's small—it doesn't mind with me." I snuggled her.

"Thank you, my rabbit," I said. "I think you're pretty amazing to see things that way, even though it's hard." Even though I wasn't sure that she would feel that way a day from now, and it was certainly not how she would always feel. Even though she was young enough not to be as hard-hit as Zanny. Whom I needed to check on now. I asked Pru if she would like to be the first tree decorator. She jumped at it, and I climbed the stairs.

Zanny was slumped on her bed, head down on the mattress. I sat next to her.

"It's hard, poodle," I said finally. Zanny raised her head and glared at me.

"I *hate* this Christmas! It's so terrible! I thought it would be fun, but it *isn't*! Our Christmas music isn't even the same!" I nodded.

"When we go downstairs, we can put on the music that you're used to," I said, praying that I could find it on some free download site. She jerked upright, wiping her face.

"It's not just *that*," she spat. "*Nothing* is the same—we can't even find my stocking! I don't know why everything has to *be* like this— it's so *hard*!" I felt a black bolt rip from my head into my gut. I scooped her up, held her, and then stroked her hair.

"This Christmas *is* really hard. It is hard for you guys, it is hard for me, and it is hard for Daddy," I said. "This will be the hardest one because everything is so different and strange. It doesn't seem like it now, but every year will get easier."

"Why is it hard for *you*?" Zanny howled. "*You're* the one who wanted things like this." That was more than I could bear. *Nobody* had wanted this, I said, my voice trembling—nobody would *ever* want this. This was the *last* thing Daddy and I ever wanted to happen, and we were *both* incredibly sad, especially because of how much it hurt her and her sister, but also because we had been best friends for almost *twenty* years. Then why, she cried, did we *do* it?

What was I doing? How could I answer that? How could I?

I heard myself saying this: Daddy and I are best friends, but we do not have a husband and wife relationship. And if you do not have a husband and wife relationship, you cannot be married—that's just how it works.

Zanny thought about this. If we didn't have a husband and wife relationship, she asked, then why had we gotten married in the first place? We had thought, I replied, that we did. So, she said, how do you know whether someone is your best friend or your husband?

It's very tricky because they can seem kind of the same, I said—sometimes you just don't know for a long time. I looked at her. But let me tell you something, my bunny, I said. Just because we cannot be married does not mean that Daddy and I don't love each other; we always have and we always will. And I think Daddy is the most perfect father there is, and I always will. And we love being your parents, and we always will. It is hard now, but it won't always be so hard. Zanny's brow relaxed, and she unfolded her arms.

"It still doesn't feel like Christmas," she said. I agreed. "But you know what? I bet it didn't feel like Christmas on the first Christmas either," I thought aloud. "Mary was poor and young and she wasn't married and she didn't know what was going to happen to her. And then she had to have her baby all alone in a barn surrounded by animals. Think about that—how scary and hard that would be. But Mary found a way to be happy at the same time."

"Yeah, but at least *she* had something to look forward to," said Zanny. "She had all those wise men coming with all those presents." I laughed, though it wasn't funny because she hadn't meant it to be funny. I hugged my little Zanny.

"You know what? I hate to say it, but I don't think all that stuff actually happened," I said, surprising myself. "I don't think there were any wise men or shepherds or presents—I think it was just Mary alone in the barn, delivering her first baby, and realizing that her little schmushkie coming into the world was the most miraculous thing that had ever happened. *That* was Christmas." Zanny considered, turning her head around in my lap.

"But the star was definitely there," she said. Then all of a sudden I remembered something that had happened when Cal and I first learned that I was pregnant with Zanny. After the doctor's appointment in which we had seen our fishy baby girl darting around in utero via the ultrasound screen, Cal and I had played hooky and gone to the Hayden Planetarium. Dwarfed under the giant dome, looking up into the eternal night of space, I had listened to Tom Hanks narrating the story of red giants and black holes and had been filled with dread and sadness: It would all come to nothing. But then a frothy, light cloud appeared, filled with cheerful-looking little fluff-balls: a star nursery! Millions of new stars were born in celestial birthplaces like this, said Tom Hanks—it was happening all the time, all over the universe. When we walked out of the planetarium, I was beaming. I had a star *inside*.

When I told her this, Zanny smiled. We walked downstairs. Pru was festooning the tree with red baubles. *Look!* she crowed. *Isn't it pretty?*

EPILOGUE:
YOU MAY FIND YOURSELF

I met my boyfriend after Cal and I split, during the worst of the worst, Kevin's and mine. It was tough, but now it isn't, even though we can barely afford to heat the house. "You know who we are?" he said to me this Christmas. "We're the Whos in Whoville—we have Christmas anyway." Kevin does antiques restoration and upscale woodworking, and he works in the garage of the house, which he refurbished as a shop. He is funny, tall, and huge-hearted, and his family background is remarkably similar to mine. Sometimes that can look like a problem, but I don't feel it as a problem because I understand it. I'm the same way. God, what a jerk he can be. What a jerk I can be. He's wonderful with my children. The night before last, they went out into the backyard and made ice cream in the snow.

Even though he is from Los Angeles, he has raised chickens his entire life. In the spring, he's building a chicken coop in the backyard, and he has approved Zanny's and Pru's bid for two hens that lay blue eggs. I'm okay with it, so long as the three of them are in charge. Plus, *blue* eggs!

My hair has finally grown out.

By accident, last year, I became pregnant. Everything got dark again. I could not do this to Zanny and Pru. I could not put them through *one more thing*. So I waited, prayed, waited. Every time I considered ending the pregnancy, something hard and deep pushed up against the thought. But how could I *do* this—how could I have a *baby*? Then an answer alighted: Because you are its mother. You are your babies' mother. And they are your soul's delight.

I had to tell Cal. I thought I would die, that it would hurt him more than almost anything else. I dreamed about it. It was always hovering over me when I was awake. Finally, I just did it, sobbing and frantic. He asked first if I had been to a doctor. Then he said: "That's going to be a lucky baby, Susie."

It is really snowing for the first time this year. Next week, it's Christmas. We are having a boy.

Telling my girls was the hardest thing I have ever done. Their response was riven into two distinct halves. First, they were thrilled, jumping up and down, at the news that they were going to have a baby brother. Second, they were devastated that their dad was not the father. They did not understand why I couldn't choose. Without getting into the mechanics of the thing, I said that while families are all different, the one thing that is the same is that to make a baby, a man has to give a woman a special seed, which implants inside her. This is just how it is. Nothing in the world can change that Daddy is your father; he just is. Many times, I've wished that my stepfather (whom my children consider their grandfather) was my father, but he isn't; my dad is my father. You can't change who your father is any more than you can change a hamster into a dog. But it's not this baby's fault. He loves us even though he hasn't even seen us yet. We all hugged on the creaky old settee for a long time.

The girls' main concern became that he not think of himself as a "half" brother. "He'll find out when he's older anyway, but I don't think we should tell him when he's little," Zanny said. "It will hurt his feelings, and plus, he *is* our real brother anyway." Months later, Pru had an oddly understandable question: If Daddy got married again, would you still be my mother? Of course, I said. Nothing in this world could make me not your mother. Even if you died? she asked. My dad died, I said, but he's still my dad. Well, said Pru, if Daddy ever had a new wife, and she stuffed me inside her uterus and gave birth to me again, would you still be my mother? I howled. Listen, rabbit face, I said, the whole world could blow up—the whole universe could blow up—and I would still be your mother. Good, she said. Because I don't want anyone else to be my mama. Well, you could not *possibly* have another mama, so don't worry about it, I said.

Money is terrifyingly scarce. The questions keep coming up; we keep talking them out. But I never say to Zanny and Pru that while divorce is difficult, everyone is happier in the end, and I will never say it. Because it isn't true. It is a horror. What we say is: Life is hard, and life is sweet. It is both things at once. Sometimes it is one more than the other, but it is always both. There is one thing that is immutable: love.

I wanted them to have something tangible to represent this reality. I struck a bargain with a jewelry maker to make the three of us necklaces with pendants of very tiny uncut diamonds. Do you know how these are made in nature? I said, holding them up in the sun one afternoon as we sat on the shore of the East River near our house. They start out as a yucky lump of charcoal, and then they are scorched by the hottest possible molten lava, and after they are burned and burned, they cool into diamonds. They are brilliant and beautiful and the toughest surface of all. So look at that: sweet and hard. Right, guys? They spent the rest of the afternoon scratching rocks on the beach with their little diamonds. Of course.

My boyfriend and I went in for the big twenty-week sonogram at the hospital, two weeks late. In the darkened delivery room, a grandmotherly technician smoothed the device over my belly, whose mysteries were revealed on a big screen on the wall. Shadowy, three-dimensional images of our son rippled by: a kicking little leg; two tiny feet; a bum. My boyfriend and I laughed and squeezed hands.

Intent on getting a closer look at his head and face, the technician suddenly stopped and punched a key on the computer to freeze the image on the screen.

"Look!" she said. "Look at him!"

Panicked, we froze, too. What, what—was there something wrong? *No,* she said, *look at his face.* We looked.

He was smiling.

ACKNOWLEDGMENTS

Limitations of space and memory often conspire to make it difficult to thank everyone you want to thank for supporting the effort of writing a book. With a book like this, however, it's flat-out impossible: If I had my way, the thanks would be longer than my kooky life story itself (they won't let me do that).

With that in mind, I am particularly grateful to my beloved friend and agent, Tina Bennett; Millicent Bennett, this book's first editor, and Svetlana Katz (Tina's right arm) for their devotion, careful thinking, and brilliance. Kate Medina, Random House's executive editorial director and associate publisher, called when I was seven months pregnant and had less than one hundred dollars in the bank to say that she loved this book; I'll never forget it. And thanks to my editor, Lindsey Schwoeri, for valiantly seeing this through to the end.

I'm damned lucky to have good friends. Say what you will about Facebook, but the comfort that friends (and "friends") sent over that mojo wire was often life-saving. My thanks especially to foxhole vets: Aunt Heather; Masha; Yuko, Jude; Barbara; the core crew at the Brooklyn Writers Space; Natileh; Anita; Colin; Jeff; Peg; Ben; Aunt Joanie; Aunt Hannah; and Howard and Linda Moss. Miss Russell—no words.

I'd have sunk were it not for my mother and stepfather. I still love my dad anyway.

T: Thank you for the days.

Mostly, I am grateful for my little crew of five: J and the schmushkies. My beautiful babies. I love you with all my heart—and even more than that.

ABOUT THE AUTHOR

SUSAN GREGORY THOMAS is a writer, journalist, and author of *Buy, Buy Baby: How Consumer Culture Manipulates Parents and Harms Young Minds*. Formerly senior editor of *US News & World Report*, Thomas has written for *The Washington Post, Time,* Babble.com, MSNBC.com, *Glamour,* and more. She lives in Brooklyn with her three children (and chickens, dog, and parrot).

ABOUT THE TYPE

This book was set in Sabon, a typeface designed by the well-known German typographer Jan Tschichold (1902–74). Sabon's design is based upon the original letter forms of Claude Garamond and was created specifically to be used for three sources: foundry type for hand composition, Linotype, and Monotype. Tschichold named his typeface for the famous Frankfurt typefounder Jacques Sabon, who died in 1580.